Christian A. Schwarz

The 3 Colors of Your Gifts

How to discover and utilize your God-given potential

Updated and revised edition 2017

NCD DISCIPLESHIP RESOURCES

NCD America

The 3 Colors of Your Gifts is one of eight books that will be published in the *NCD Discipleship Resources* series. Each book covers one of the eight quality characteristics of healthy communities.

The basic introduction to the latest generation of Natural Church Development (NCD 3.0):

Christian A. Schwarz
The All By Itself Pathway
Paperback, 96 pages, fully illustrated, with 25 full-color photos and diagrams

Resources on the theory and practice of natural church development are available in about 40 languages. Titles and ordering information can be found on the Internet at:
www.ncd-international.org
www.ncdamerica.org

Retail price $19.95 – Quantity discounts available
Call 1-888-8forNCD for current pricing or check www.ncdamerica.org

Published by NCD America
Berrien Springs, MI 49104

Fifth, updated and revised edition 2017

© 2001 by Christian A. Schwarz
NCD Media, Emmelsbüll, Germany

© U.S.A. edition: 2017 by NCD America
4145 E Campus Circle Dr, Berrien Springs, MI 49104
info@ncdamerica.org

Edited by Jon & Kathy Haley

Scripture taken from *Holy Bible: New International Version*®
© 1973, 1978, 1984 by International Bible Society. Used by permission of Zondervan Publishing House. All rights reserved.

Printing: Mohndruck GmbH, Gütersloh • Printed in Germany

ISBN 978-0-9987021-0-0

THE 3 COLORS OF YOUR GIFTS

WHAT YOU CAN EXPECT FROM THIS BOOK

One highly encouraging result when surveying people who have taken previous versions of the *Three-Color Gift Test* was that 51% indicated that they have become "happier" as a result. This number increased to 72% when the discovered gifts were applied to concrete ministries. There is hardly another factor that has a stronger bearing on perceived happiness than living in line with the spiritual gifts that God has imparted to every single one of us.

What does it mean, in practical terms, to be a part of the body of Christ? And what visible changes take place in our lives, as a result of being part of the body of Christ? That is the actual topic of this book—the discovery of our spiritual gifts is merely a means to this end.

THOUSANDS OF PEOPLE HAVE TOLD US THAT GOD HAS USED THIS TOOL TO SHOW THEM THEIR UNIQUE CALLING.

CONNECTING TO THE E-WORLD

In previous editions, the *Three-Color Gift Test* was supplied in paper form, printed on 23 pages within this book. Throughout the past few years, we have increasingly been urged...

- to offer the ***Three-Color Gift Test* separately** from the book in order to help people discover their gifts, even if they are not (yet) willing to study a whole book;

- to offer the test in a more **automated format** which produces the results through a simple mouse click, rather than asking people to use pen or pencil while going through long questionnaires and normation tables;

- to offer the test **online** in order to make full use of the interactivity of the e-world and to produce profiles that go far beyond the identification of three or five spiritual gifts;

- to offer substantial **discounts for groups** that plan to take the *Three-Color Gift Test* with the goal of enabling a whole church or all the participants of a conference to take the test.

After huge investments in a web based, international infrastructure we are happy that we can finally offer the *Three-Color Gift Test* as online eTest.

ADVANTAGES OF THE ONLINE VERSIONS

The availability of this eTest (see page 69) gives people who want to discover their spiritual gifts, or help others to do so, a number of advantages:

1. From now on, this tool (just as the other *NCD Discipleship Resources*) is available in **three different forms**: as paperback, as eBook (both containing the tokens for the eTests), and as pure eTests. You can decide which "delivery channel" is most helpful in your specific context.

2. Taking the eTest works considerably **quicker and easier** than it was possible at the time of the print-version of the test.

3. People who exclusively would like to identify their three or five strongest developed spiritual gifts—and nothing else—will still get this basic information and are free to disregard the additional possibilities that the online version offers. However, the online evaluation enables a wide spectrum of **advanced and far more nuanced insights** into one's gift profile.

4. Since we have now, for the first time, all results (in all language versions in which the book has been published) online, we can develop much **more precise normations** and can update them automatically, resulting in more precise test results.

5. The extensive group discounts for the eTest make it considerably easier to use the *Three-Color Gift Test* in the context of small or **large groups** of people.

6. With just some additional mouse clicks it is now possible to produce a **group profile** once a sufficient number of participants have taken the test, for instance the gift profile of a small group, a local church, or a specific leadership team (see page 72).

ONCE YOU HAVE PUT INTO PRACTICE THE STEPS SUGGESTED IN THIS BOOK, YOU CAN EXPECT TO BE A HAPPIER PERSON.

7. It has become possible not just to work with two "external questionnaires" (as was the case at the time of the print-version). Rather, you can now easily **invite as many people as you want to fill in an online questionnaire** for you. That will result in more meaningful results.

8. With just a few mouse clicks you can easily **share your results** with people from whom you would like to get feedback—together with the three previous points this is a decisive step to prevent the gift discovery process from becoming an entirely individualistic exercise.

SPIRITUAL GIFTS AND COMMUNITY

Strictly speaking, spiritual gifts are not given to individual believers, but to the "body of Christ," which is, to the community. Therefore both the discovery and the implementation of gifts should be a collaborative enterprise. We have stressed this principle even in previous editions of the book, but since in the past there have been no technical possibilities to practically integrate the communal aspect into the gift discovery process, this teaching didn't have dramatic consequences, to put it mildly.

For me, this theological aspect (i.e. gift discovery not as a individualistic enterprise, but as a task of the body of Christ as a whole) is the most important benefit of the online procedure that some people may perceive as a mere technical feature. When we take into account that the NCD

Community is represented in more than 70 countries, encompassing most diverse churches, spiritual traditions, and cultures, with which we can have growth-stimulating communication, we may realize that now, for the first time, we can put into practice a spiritual principle that goes back to the New Testament, but had only limited practical applicability for individual believers—namely the experience of Christianity as *oikumene*, i.e. as the body of Christ represented throughout the whole inhabited world.

GIFTS ARE NOT GIVEN TO INDIVIDUALS, BUT TO THE BODY OF CHRIST, WHICH IS, TO THE COMMUNITY.

Since all language editions of the *NCD Discipleship Resources* follow exactly the same scheme (which means that in other languages than English the graphic on page 16 in any foreign language edition is exactly the same as the graphic on page 16 in your book, just with Korean/Norwegian/German etc. terms), it is possible for Russians and Americans, Finns and Chinese, Brazilians and Greeks to speak exactly the same "three-color language"—independent of the denomination or stream they may be affiliated with. This enables a way of ecumenical learning that had not been possible in the past.

THREE MEANINGS OF NCD

The acronym NCD has originally been coined as a shortcut for *Natural Church Development*—and this will remain a key focus of our ministry at NCD International: applying principles that we could learn from our international research to the realities of local churches and whole denominations. However, throughout the past 20 years we have increasingly seen the necessity to render the "C" in NCD in two additional ways, as *Character* and *Community*. "Church" Development, properly understood, is nothing other than both character development and community development. In NCD we neither develop the quality of pipe organs nor the health of church pews, but the quality and health of the people sitting in the pews.

This refocus of what church development is all about has dramatic consequences for every reader of this book. Don't wait for the pastors or elders of your local church to take the initiative in terms of gift discovery. It is your responsibility to live out the potential that God has planted in your life. While working on your own *character* and on the *community* around you, you make the most effective contribution to *church* development at the same time. And even if your local church, for whatever reasons, may not be open to your specific contribution, nobody can stop you putting your God-given potential into practice.

ENJOYING THE UNFAMILIAR

It could be that a number of terms and concepts used in this book may be unfamiliar to you, for instance the labels for some of the spiritual gifts, or the way some gifts are defined. And maybe you have the impression that some of the topics covered in this book don't really apply to you. However, keep in mind that this book has an international and interdenominational background. All phenomena described do exist—maybe not in your life, but in the lives of other people; maybe not in your group or church, but in other groups or churches; maybe not in your culture, but in other cultures. This book has not been designed to make you "similar to the others," but to release the potential that God has planted in your own life. In this process, the communication with other people who have gained different experiences can be of enormous help.

In short, whenever you encounter, while reading this book, a certain feature that seems to be strange to you, don't get angry. Simply see it as an indication of the cultural and spiritual diversity of the worldwide body of Christ. In the past, the possibilities for mutual learning had been extremely limited, simply because the chance for meaningful encounters with people representing different cultures have been limited. In our increasingly globalized world, this has changed dramatically. I would like to encourage you to see this as a privilege. At no time in history has spiritual learning been as easy as it is today. It is up to you what you make out of it.

THE THINGS THAT DIDN'T CHANGE

With all of the changes that have taken place in the world around you, what are the things that have not changed?

Surprisingly or not, it is the New Testament teaching on spiritual gifts. In this regard, not a single *iota* changed—aside from the fact that this teaching may today be even more relevant than at the time of its origination. Thousands of people who have worked with predecessor versions of this book have told us that God has used this tool to show them their unique calling—and that this has made them both happier and more effective within their local churches. And more importantly, it has made them more effective in their ministry to the world, far beyond the borders of their local church.

NCD International   *Christian A. Schwarz*

ONLINE ETEST

Each copy of this book includes a bookmark with an individual access code. When you enter the code on the web site **www.ncd-tools.org/mycode** *you can take the Three-Color Gift Test online. In addition, the access code activates a second online test of your choice, which is a gift from us. You will find all needed instructions on the web site.*

WHAT ARE THE 3 COLORS OF MINISTRY?

At many Christian conferences I have heard it said, "What we urgently need is a new level of dedication among Christians," which sounds as if increasing our personal commitment were the key to all of our problems. Among other Christians the motto is, "The only thing that can change the state of our churches is supernatural power." And a third group teaches, "If we Christians simply acted more wisely, we would probably be amazed at how many problems would disappear." Well, who is right? In a way, all of them are right, and in another way, none of them are right. The simple truth is this: The very thing that might be "right" for some Christians would be completely misleading for others. Not all Christians need more commitment, but some do. Not all Christians need more power, but some do. Not all Christians need more wisdom, but some do. How can we discover what is the greatest need in our own lives?

CHAPTER 1:

THREE WAYS TO EXPERIENCE GOD

D o you have the impression that you already understand God's nature? Are you convinced that you really experience the "fullness of life" that the New Testament promises? Do you think that your church lives 100 percent according to God's plan and that there is no need even to think about changing directions?

If you have answered "yes" to these questions, I first want to congratulate you, and second, I would like to say "good bye" to you. This book has not been written for you. It has been written for people who are striving constantly to grow in their understanding of God—rationally, emotionally, and socially. It has been written for those who dare to reconsider the answers that they have found so far, and who are open to learn new things about God, about the church, and about themselves.

MANY CHRISTIANS ARE ACQUAINTED ONLY WITH CERTAIN ASPECTS OF GOD'S NATURE, AND NEW DISCOVERIES ARE WAITING FOR THEM.

THE CENTER OF THE CHRISTIAN FAITH

In this book (as well as in the other *NCD Discipleship Resources*), I don't want to speak to you about certain fringe issues of theology, but about the center of our Christian faith—the one God who has revealed himself in three different ways: as Creator, in Jesus, and in the Holy Spirit. Look at the diagram to the right. As pure white light shining through a prism refracts into the different colors of the spectrum, so God has revealed different aspects of his nature in three major revelations: Creation (green segment), Calvary (red segment), and Pentecost (blue segment). The dilemma of Christianity is that, while we might give intellectual assent to this threefold revelation, when it comes to everyday practical experience, most of us are miles from integrating all three dimensions into our personal lives. There are some Christians who seem exclusively to see red, others only blue, and others only green. And if we have a limited understanding of God, we are in danger of portraying only limited aspects of God's nature in our lives and churches.

A SEGMENTED FAITH

In my own ministry in very different denominations and cultures, I have encountered purely "green" churches as well as purely "red" and purely "blue" ones. Sometimes I find combinations of two of the colors—how wonderful!—but very seldom do I find a truly "three-colored," trinitarian church: totally *Christ-centered,* stressing the claims of Jesus, and inviting people to find a personal relationship with him (red segment); living in the *power of the Holy Spirit,* not only teaching about, but experiencing the transrational dimension of our faith (blue segment); and all of this based on principles that God has revealed to us in *creation* that we share with nonbelievers, which include striving for the preservation of creation, social justice, human rights, and peace (green segment). I am convinced that most of the problems that we face, in the final anal-

Creator

God

Spirit

Jesus

According to the Bible, God has revealed himself in three different ways: as Creator (green segment), in Jesus (red segment), and in the Holy Spirit (blue segment). Each of these three revelations corresponds to a specific way in which we can experience God. Problems start as soon as we emphasize one of the three "colors" and neglect the others.

ysis, have their roots in our limited understanding of the triune God. This is a rather frustrating situation!

CHANGE IS POSSIBLE

But here comes the good news. I have seen again and again that this situation can be changed. Regardless of the condition of a person or a church right now (emphasizing the green, red, or blue segment), it is possible to integrate the other colors as well. I have seen totally "green" churches (with all their limitations and dangers) moving more and more into the "red" and the "blue" dimensions, and I have seen "blue" and "red" churches expanding their ministry into the "green" area, thus experiencing growth in their effectiveness.

Look at the diagram above. If one wanted to describe the starting points of these churches, it would be necessary to draw three circles: one in the green segment, another in the red, and another in the blue. There is only one circle that can encompass all three colors, and that would be a circle around the center. This is a metaphor for the journey that I would like to invite you to take. Wherever your starting point might be, the nearer you draw to the center, the more you will radiate all three colors.

GOAL: THE THREE-COLOR CHRISTIAN

The three colors stand for three different dimensions of life. Our goal should be to invite God into each of these areas, at which point we become "Three-Color Christians." This term does not refer to any "perfect" state that would be unrealistic to achieve. The Three-Color Christian will not always radiate all of the three colors, but he or she will deeply desire to do so. We will only experience greater fruitfulness if all three dimensions are integrated into our lives.

ARE YOU A THREE-COLOR CHRISTIAN?

THE THREE-COLOR CHRISTIAN WILL NOT ALWAYS RADIATE ALL OF THE THREE COLORS, BUT HE OR SHE WILL DEEPLY DESIRE TO DO SO.

If you want to find out if you are already a Three-Color Christian, it is helpful to check a variety of areas. It might be that in some areas of your life you are typically "blue," while in other areas, you show more "red" or "green." For starters, look at the six diagrams at the bottom of this double page. Each of them represents one aspect of reality (I could add literally hundreds of further examples) and shows the specific "green," "red," and "blue" dimensions of the issue under consideration.

We have already dealt with the *first diagram,* the three works of God: Creation (green segment), Calvary (red segment), and Pentecost (blue segment). For most Christians, one or two of these three works have more importance than the others. This is normal. However, we must never allow any of these three works to be excluded from our Christian experience.

Look at the *second diagram,* which describes three dimensions of life. The ancient Greeks referred to this as body (green segment), soul (red segment), and spirit (blue segment). One could argue whether separating life into these three dimensions is really "Christian," or "Greek." My answer would be that any separation is not Christian. Rather, integrating all three dimensions is the biblical goal. Is any one of the three dimensions more important to you than the others?

3 WORKS OF GOD **3 DIMENSIONS OF LIFE** **3 CONVERSIONS**

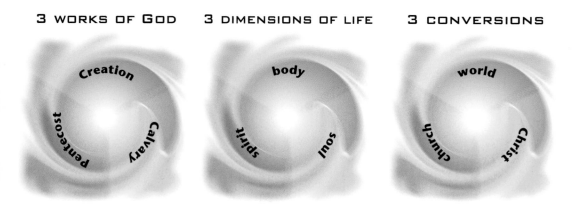

Now turn to the *third diagram.* Nicolaus Zinzendorf, one of the fathers of Pietism, and therefore of the evangelical movement today, taught that every Christian needs three "conversions": first, a conversion from the world to Christ (red segment); second, a conversion to the church (blue segment); and third, a conversion back to the world (green segment). If this final stage is not reached, people will probably not be very effective in their ministry to the world. Where would you say you are in your spiritual development?

WE WILL ONLY EXPERIENCE GREATER FRUITFULNESS IF ALL THREE DIMENSIONS ARE INTEGRATED INTO OUR LIVES.

The *fourth diagram* shows three authorities: science (green segment), Scripture (red segment), and experience (blue segment). Each of them is important, and none of them must be downgraded or excluded—even if they don't all have the same value. Which of these authorities is really decisive in your daily life?

In the *fifth diagram* I have listed three tendencies that we find in worldwide Christianity. Is it really a coincidence that each of them has a special affinity for one of the three colors? Liberals advocate the creation revelation (green segment), evangelicals advocate the salvation revelation (red segment), and charismatics advocate the personal revelation (blue segment). Do you feel more comfortable in one of these groups than in the others?

And finally, the *sixth diagram* describes the specific dangers of the three groups mentioned above: the danger of liberals would be "syncretism" (green segment), the danger of evangelicals, "dogmatism" (red segment), and the danger of charismatics, "spiritualism" (blue segment). By this statement I don't mean that every evangelical tends toward dogmatism, every liberal is syncretistic, etc. However, these dangers exist as soon as one of the three elements is isolated from the other two. Heresy is not necessarily the opposite of truth; very often it is something

3 AUTHORITIES   **3 TENDENCIES**   **3 DANGERS**

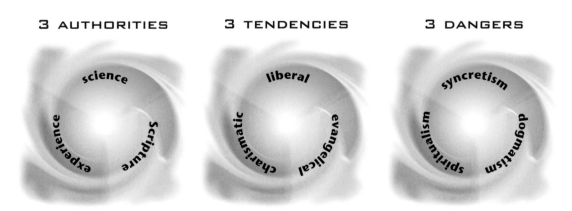

The background of the three colors being used in this book are God's major acts in history: the "creation revelation" (green segment), symbolized by the rainbow; the "salvation revelation" (red segment), symbolized by the cross; and the "personal revelation" (blue segment), symbolized by the dove.

far more subtle—a partial truth. Have you ever encountered one of the three dangers described here?

TOWARD A BALANCED BIBLICAL FAITH

Creation, Calvary, and Pentecost—all of them are indispensable for a healthy, balanced, biblical faith. Let me exaggerate a little bit to make my point clear. There are people for whom only God's revelation in creation seems to constitute what is important in Christianity; for others, it is exclusively Calvary; for others again, exclusively Pentecost. Each of these groups is right in fighting for its specific agenda, but wrong in positioning it against the other groups.

In this book I would like to invite you to become a truly Three-Color Christian: empowered (blue segment), committed (red segment), and wise (green segment). Can this happen? Of course, it can! This is exactly God's desire for every believer.

THREE DIMENSIONS OF MINISTRY

How does all of this relate to gift-based ministry? If we approach this subject from the perspective that there is one God who has revealed himself in three different ways, the consequences are far-reaching. Each of the three colors corresponds to one dimension of ministry. It is essential for all of us to find out in which of these three areas we are already strong, and in which areas we need further growth.

POWER PLUS COMMITMENT PLUS WISDOM IS THE KEY TO A FRUITFUL LIFE.

GIFTS AND THE TRINITY

In 1 Corinthians 12:4–6, Paul introduces a truly "trinitarian" view of spiritual gifts. "There are different kinds of gifts," he writes, "but the same Spirit. There are different kinds of service, but the same Lord. There are different kinds of energies, but the same God works all of them in all men."

In the diagram at the bottom of this page you can see how these verses relate to the three colors, blue, red, and green. Spiritual *gifts* are related to the *Holy Spirit* (blue area). *Service* is related to the *Lord,* a term that in New Testament usage usually refers to Jesus (red area). The third term is a little more difficult to grasp: the *energies* (many Bible translations use the imprecise term "workings;" the literal rendering of the Greek term *energemata* would be be "effects of energy") is related to *God.* Put into the terminology we have used so far, this would be God the Creator and thus belong to the green area. It should be noted that the whole idea of this passage is not to separate these three dimensions, but to stress that they belong inextricably together. Problems start as soon as we isolate one of these dimensions from the others.

THE UNDERLYING CONCEPT

At first sight all of this might seem rather abstract, but as soon as we look at the concept behind the three colors, it becomes eminently practical. In order to describe these concepts, I have chosen the terms *power, commitment,* and *wisdom.* "Power" is related to the area of spiritual gifts (blue segment); "commitment," to the area of service (red segment); and "wisdom," to the area of creation (green segment).

1 Corinthians 12: 4–6 describes three dimensions (gifts, service, energies) and how they relate to the triune God.

There are different kinds of **gifts**, but the same **Spirit**.	**Spirit** ➡ **gifts**	**power**
There are different kinds of **service**, but the same **Lord**.	**Jesus** ➡ **service**	**commitment**
There are different kinds of **energies**, but the same **God**.	**Creator** ➡ **energies**	**wisdom**

This diagram shows the three dimensions of ministry (power, commitment, and wisdom) and how they relate to the three colors blue, red, and green. Depending on your present starting point, you can determine what you most need in order to become more effective in ministry. For some, the greatest need is empowerment; for others, commitment; and for still others it is wisdom.

On pages 22–24 we will take a closer look at these three terms and what they mean in the Bible. Right now, my goal is simply to show you the central importance of a trinitarian approach to the subject of gift-based ministry.

The diagram at the top of this page transfers these concepts to the

This diagram shows that "gifts/power" and "service/commitment" form two poles that must be related to each other. What brings them together properly is the "wisdom" found in the green segment, in other words, in God's creation.

trinitarian diagram that we have been using throughout the first few pages of this book. The small diagram (left) shows that "gifts/power" and "service/commitment" form two poles. Power without commitment is useless, but commitment without power is fruitless. Gift-based ministry simply means that gifts and service, organism and organization, left pole and right pole, blue color and red color, are related to each other. And now comes the interesting discovery: What brings both poles together properly is the "wisdom" found in the green segment.

THE MOST IMPORTANT ASPECT

What, then, is the most important aspect for your life: power, commitment, or wisdom? The answer to this question exclusively depends on what your starting point is.

Are you already strong in power and wisdom, but weak in commitment? Or are you strong in commitment and wisdom, but lacking spiritual power? Or are you among those dedicated Christians who are strong in both power and commitment, but need to concentrate on wisdom? If you find the answer to these questions, you will know the direction that your spiritual journey should take.

The reality behind the three colors of ministry is an issue packed with practical relevance. The Bible describes again and again how these three dimensions interrelate. A beautiful example of this is Colossians 1:9–11, where Paul summarizes his prayers for the church in Colosse: "For this reason, since the day we heard about you, we have not stopped praying for you and asking God to fill you with the knowledge of his will through all spiritual wisdom and understanding. And we pray this in order that you may live a life worthy of the Lord and may please him in every way: bearing fruit in every good work, growing in the knowledge of God, being strengthened with all power according to his glorious might." As you can see in the diagram at the bottom of this page, all three "colors" are clearly evident in this passage.

According to some people, the key to success is spiritual power; for others it is commitment; and for still others, wisdom. Without a doubt, power plus commitment plus wisdom is the key to a fruitful life.

ACCORDING TO SOME, THE KEY TO SUCCESS IS SPIRITUAL POWER; FOR OTHERS, COMMITMENT; AND FOR STILL OTHERS, WISDOM.

Colossians 1:9–11 is another example of the central importance of the three dimensions in ministry.

For this reason ... we have not stopped praying for you and asking God ...	**Prayer for:**
... to fill you with the knowledge of his will through all spiritual wisdom and understanding ...	• **wisdom**
... that you may live a life worthy of the Lord and may please him in every way: bearing fruit in every good work, growing in the knowledge of God, ...	• **commitment**
... being strengthened with all power according to his glorious might.	• **power**

THE DIVINE "ENÉRGEIA"

P ossibly you were surprised that, in the last chapter, 1 Corinthians 12:4–6 was translated like this: "There are different kinds of gifts, but the same Spirit. There are different kinds of service, but the same Lord. There are different kinds of energies, but the same God." Rather than speaking about energies, most English Bible translations use, in this and other contexts, terms like "workings," "forces," "powers," or simply "effects," which is not wrong, but can explain why we are familiar with concepts like "spiritual gifts" and the "fruit of the Spirit," but not with the concept of the "divine energies." I have frequently experienced that, when I used this term, some Christians believed I was referring to a concept that is foreign to the Bible.

SINCE TERMS LIKE *ENERGEIA* AND *ENERGEO* HAVE NOT BEEN TRANSLATED BY *ENERGY* OR *ENERGIZE*, MANY PEOPLE ARE NOT AWARE THAT WE ARE SPEAKING ABOUT A CORE BIBLICAL CONCEPT.

SCRIPTURE ON DIVINE ENERGIES

However, "energy" is a key term in Scripture. In the Greek New Testament, it is expressed in different ways: *energeia* and *energema* (nouns), *energes* (adjective) and *energeo* (verb).

Have a look at the green box to the right. In this box I have selected a few Bible verses on energies which are of great relevance for our topic—the dynamics of the body of Christ. Just imagine if, in all of these cases, the translators had decided to speak about "energies" and "energize"—rather than "workings" and "work." The concept of the divine energies would today be a completely undisputed category within Christianity.

THE NATURE OF ENERGIES

From physics, many are familiar with the principle of energy conservation. In nature, we can detect many different kinds

Example for the results of the Communal Test, which is part of the book "The 3 Colors of Community" and also available as an eTest. The test reveals how strongly each of the seven energies manifests itself in a person's life. People with high energy for identity have great potential to help others identify and develop their gifts.

Energy for:	
Empowerment	power
Effectiveness	pleasure
Gift-activation	identity
Need-relief	sustenance
Love	justice
Passion	renewal
Inspiration	intimacy

1 Corinthians 12:6: *"There are different varieties of workings (ἐνεργη-μάτων); but the same God who works (ἐνεργῶν) all things in all persons."*

Ephesians 3:7: *"... of which I was made a minister, according to the gift of God's grace which was given to me according to the working (ἐνέργειαν) of his power."*

Ephesians 4:16: *"... from whom the whole body, being fitted and held together by what every joint supplies, according to the proper working (ἐνέργειαν) of each individual part, causes the growth of the body for the building up of itself in love."*

Philippians 2:13: *"For it is God who works (ἐνεργῶν) in you to will and to act (ἐνεργεῖν) according to his good purpose."*

Colossians 1:29: *"For this purpose also I labor, striving according to his power (ἐνέργειαν) which mightily works (ενεργουμένην) within me."*

Some of many New Testament statements on "energies." Since in English Bibles the corresponding Greek term has hardly ever been translated as "energy," for most churches the concept of the divine energies is virtually unknown.

of energies: thermal energy, electrical energy, energy of gravitation, of movement, of magnetism, etc. All of these energies together add up to the energy supply of the world. This supply is unchangeable, i.e. it can neither be increased nor diminished. "All changes that happen are, in actual fact, nothing other than mutual transformations of energy," Max Planck writes. "When for instance energy of movement gets lost through friction, the equivalent amount of thermal energy emerges."

These insights are of enormous relevance in our context of dealing with gift-based ministry. All of us only have limited energies. Therefore it is important to channel all of our existing energies in such a way that they contribute, as effectively as possible, to the kingdom of God.

HIGH IDENTITY ENERGY

Have a look at the diagram to the left. It has been taken from the book, *The 3 Colors of Community,* which deals with the practical implications of the divine *enérgeia* (including a test for identifying your energies). The book demonstrates how important it is not only to relate our *gifts* (1 Cor. 12:4) to concrete *tasks* (1 Cor. 12:5), but to do this in line with our respective energies (1 Cor. 12:6). In our context, the energy of "identity" plays an important role. People with high energy in this area have great potential to help others identify and develop their gifts. In other words, they must be seen as key players when it comes to gift-activation.

Since most Christians are not familiar with the concept of the divine energies (yet), they have difficulty understanding the exact relationship between gifts, ministries, and energies.

"ENÉRGEIA" AND SPIRITUAL GIFTS

Take a look at the diagram to the right. It illustrates the relationship between God's *enérgeia* (1), spiritual gifts (2), and ministries (3).

1. Through God's **enérgeia** we are connected to God himself. We are free to use these energies in various ways, either for selfish and destructive purposes or by investing them for the kingdom of God. Just as it applies to spiritual gifts, divine energies can be both properly used and misused. It is our decision.

2. Even when we decide to invest the energies for the kingdom of God, this can be done in a plethora of different ways and in countless areas. However, according to God's plan we should express the energies through the channel of our respective **spiritual gifts**. But even the gifts can be misused, if we fail to relate them to appropriate ministries focused on blessing others.

3. For that reason, the spiritual gifts (2) that are energized by God himself (1) must be related to concrete **ministries** (3). Following that path, we create a channel through which God's power flows freely through our lives into the lives of other people, enabling them to experience God's work in their lives.

BECOMING A CHANNEL OF GOD'S WORKING

In other words, the relationship between enérgeia, spiritual gifts, and ministries is all about finding the most adequate channel through which God's power and love can flow into the lives of other people. With each step in the diagram, there is an increase in focus so that finally people experience God's power and love in the way that God has intended. In actual fact, when people are touched by ministry that is based on spiritual gifts and empowered by God's *enérgeia*, they are touched by God himself.

In Natural Church Development, we speak about "all by itself growth"—rather than pursuing church growth in our own human strength, we strive to bring our lives in harmony with God's principles so that his Spirit can flow through us to other people. However, in each of the three steps we are free to decide whether or not we live in line with these dynamics. The "all by itself principle" only works if it finds agents that are willing to function as human channels for the Holy Spirit. As human beings, we cannot "make" these dynamics happen—it is exclusively God's work in us—but we can hinder this touch of God from taking place.

ANOINTED AND UNANOINTED MINISTRY

So far, we have looked at the diagram from left to right and discovered the dynamic of increased anointing with every step

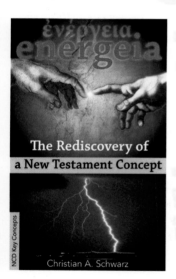

The cover of the English edition of the book presenting the New Testament concept of "enérgeia." The book also explains why this concept, in spite of the clear teaching in the Greek New Testament, had not been picked up by Western Christianity in the past.

Enérgeia, spiritual gifts, ministries: Increasing anointing with every step

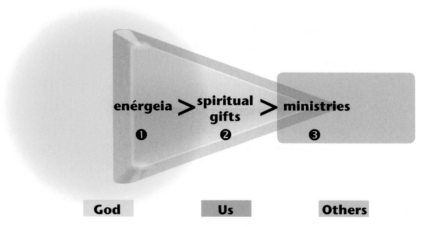

Through the divine enérgeia (1) we get access to God's power, i.e. the energies represent God's presence within us. We can express these energies most effectively through the channel of our corresponding spiritual gifts (2). These gifts must be related to fitting ministries (3), through which we bless the lives of other people.

in the sequence. Just expressing your *enérgeia* (without any focus) is less effective than expressing them through the channel of our spiritual gifts; playing around with our spiritual gifts (without any focus) is less effective than consistently applying them to real needs.

This dynamic of increasing (or decreasing) anointing becomes even more obvious when we approach the diagram from right to left. It is a widespread reality in many churches that church members are encouraged to take over ministries (3) without ever asking whether they have the corresponding spiritual gifts, and without any practical help in discovering and developing these gifts (2). These people can be wonderfully spiritually motivated, but yet they never experience the kind of fruitfulness that God had originally in mind.

Thanks to God, throughout the past few decades thousands of churches have worked on this problem by helping people relate their gifts (2) to fitting ministries (3) and providing all kind of support in that area.

RELEASING OUR FULL GOD-GIVEN POTENTIAL

But even if we have done this necessary step, we may still live far below the potential that God has planted in our lives, by ignoring the *enérgeia* through which God wants to work in us (1). Only by discovering these energies and letting them flow through the channels of spiritual gifts and corresponding ministries can we expect to release our full God-given potential. Even more, as 1 Corinthians 12:4–6 teaches us (see page 15), in all three areas it is the triune God himself who works in and through us.

CHAPTER 1: FOUNDATIONS

THE COLOR RED: COMMITMENT

The color red, as we use it in the Trinitarian Compass, reminds us of what Jesus has done for us on the cross. At the same time, it is a symbol of our commitment to him. It is not by accident that 1 Corinthians 12:4–6 clearly relates Christian "service" to "the Lord," who is Jesus. Philippians 2:5–8 describes this dimension in an unsurpassed way: "Your attitude should be the same as that of Christ Jesus: Who, being in very nature God, did not consider equality with God something to be grasped, but made himself nothing, taking the very nature of a servant, being made in human likeness. And being found in appearance as a man, he humbled himself and became obedient to death—even death on a cross."

RED REMINDS US OF WHAT JESUS HAS DONE FOR US ON THE CROSS. AT THE SAME TIME, IT IS A SYMBOL OF OUR COMMITMENT TO HIM.

TAKING UP THE CROSS

When we study the life of Jesus as described in the New Testament, we cannot escape the fact that there is no discipleship without sacrifice. Jesus taught his disciples clearly, "If anyone would come after me, he must deny himself and take up his cross and follow me. For whoever wants to save his life will lose it, but whoever loses his life for me will find it" (Matthew 16:24–25).

Following Christ is not a weekend hobby; rather, it is a costly lifestyle. It literally means sacrificing our lives to the Lord. "Therefore, I urge you, brothers, in view of God's mercy," Paul writes in his letter to the Romans, "to offer your bodies as living sacrifices, holy and pleasing to God—this is your spiritual act of worship" (Romans 12:1).

THE KEY: OBEDIENCE

Many Christians stress the importance of commitment, service, dedication, obedience, etc.—and rightly so. Without this dimension the Christian church would cease to exist. These groups worry that the church of Jesus Christ might, in its attempt to "please the world," give up the dimension of sacrificial commitment which is out of step with the rest of society. Therefore, they quote Paul's words: "Do not conform any longer to the pattern of this world, but be transformed by the renewing of your mind. Then you will be able to test and approve what God's will is—his good, pleasing and perfect will" (Romans 12:2).

COMMITMENT WITHOUT POWER AND WISDOM

While all of this is undoubtedly right and absolutely indispensable, it is not *all* that the Bible teaches about Christian ministry. You could be highly committed, but lack spiritual power; or you might be extremely dedicated to the Lord, but deficient in wisdom. If one of these situations applies to you, it will not help you to stress the dimension of commitment even more. The key to a more fruitful ministry will be found somewhere else.

THE COLOR BLUE: POWER

CHAPTER 1:
FOUNDATIONS

I n Acts 1:8, the risen Christ is quoted as follows: "You will receive power when the Holy Spirit comes on you; and you will be my witnesses in Jerusalem, and in all Judea and Samaria, and to the ends of the earth." Everyone who wants to be an effective witness for Christ depends on this power. Of course, you could try to minister without it, but you would probably not be very fruitful. Yet this is the situation of many Christians. They want to be obedient to Christ, but they sense that they literally lack "power from on high."

With regard to Jesus' ministry, there are expressions in the New Testament like "the power of the Lord was present for him to heal the sick" (Luke 5:17). If it is explicitly stated that God's power was present at that specific time, we can presume that there could have been other times when this power was not present. In Mark 6:5 we even read that Jesus, in a specific situation, *could* not do any miracles. While these statements describe Jesus' ministry and not our own, we can see that, even for him, "power" was apparently not a static possession, but something that could be present or absent.

WITHOUT POWER, NO FRUIT

The same dynamic applies all the more to us. Jesus taught his disciples that there might be times when we simply have to *wait*—a fact that those who exclusively stress the importance of commitment seem to forget. "I am going to send you what my Father has promised," Jesus said, "but stay in the city until you have been clothed with power from on high" (Luke 24:49). The concept is clear: without power there can be no fruitful ministry. To stress the importance of commitment in such a situation would be counterproductive.

There might be two Christians who do exactly the same kind of ministry, and while one is extremely fruitful, the other despairs. The difference is not necessarily the level of commitment (red area); it might simply be whether or not this commitment is accompanied by divine power (blue area).

THE BIBLE USES THE SAME TERM FOR "SPIRIT" AND "WIND." BLUE, THEN, IS A FITTING COLOR FOR THE POWER OF THE HOLY SPIRIT.

THE SYMBOL OF THE WIND

It is interesting that both in Hebrew (the language of the Old Testament) and in Greek (the language of the New Testament) the terms for "wind" and "spirit" are absolutely identical. So it is no accident that in Genesis 2:7 we read that human life literally started by God "breathing the breath of life" into the "dust of the ground." And when Jesus met his disciples for the first time after his resurrection, we learn that "he breathed on them and said, 'Receive the Holy Spirit'" (John 20:22). Thus, it seems fitting to take the color blue as a symbol of the power of the Holy Spirit.

**CHAPTER 1:
FOUNDATIONS**

THE COLOR GREEN: WISDOM

Wisdom is one of the central concepts of both the Old and the New Testaments. There is a whole category of biblical books referred to as "wisdom writings," which includes Proverbs, Ecclesiastes, and in a wider sense the Book of Job and a number of psalms. A vast part of Jesus' earthly ministry was in the tradition of an Old Testament wisdom teacher. Even Paul's teaching on God's *enérgeia* can be seen as a fruit of this wisdom tradition.

THE BIBLE TEACHES US THAT GOD MADE CREATION "BY WISDOM." GREEN IS THE SYMBOL FOR THE WISDOM THAT WE CAN FIND IN GOD'S CREATION.

The New Testament teaches us about the importance of wisdom in ministry. Colossians 4:5 admonishes us, "Be wise in the way you act toward outsiders; make the most of every opportunity." And in James 1:5 we read, "If any of you lacks wisdom, he should ask God, who gives generously to all without finding fault, and it will be given to him."

THE ESSENCE OF WISDOM

But what exactly is wisdom according to the Bible? It is knowledge applied to real life situations, which is eminently practical. The wise person in the Bible is not an abstract philosopher or speculative theoretician, but a person who can relate his or her knowledge to actual questions that people have. Wisdom is the opposite of dogmatism and ideology, thinking in black-and-white categories. To use the terminology of our three-colored diagram, ideally, wise people are able to integrate all three colors, being aware that they depend on spiritual power (blue segment), and that all wisdom must finally result in action (red segment).

HOW WISDOM CAN BE PERVERTED

I deliberately said "ideally" because this is very often not the case. Wisdom can be isolated from the other two dimensions. We can find examples of this both in the Old and the New Testaments. For instance, in many cases where Paul uses this term, it has a rather critical connotation. If you study these passages in greater detail, you will discover that what Paul criticizes is never wisdom as described above, but always a concept of wisdom that isolates itself either from spiritual power or commitment, or from both.

WISDOM AND CREATION

The biblical concept of wisdom is intimately related to creation. The Bible teaches us that God made creation "by wisdom" (Proverbs 3:19). As it has its roots in creation, wisdom is not an exclusively "Christian" business. Nonbelievers can have wisdom as well. In the Old Testament, wisdom is something international and interreligious. 1 Kings 4:30 quite openly states that there was wisdom outside of Israel, for example, in Egypt and among the "men of the East." If we want to grow in wisdom, there is much for us to learn even outside the Christian context.

WHAT IS YOUR PERSONAL COLOR BLEND?

The message of this book is quite simple. Are you lacking power? Discover your *spiritual gifts*. Is commitment your weakness? Relate your gifts to concrete *services*. Have you done this and still find that your ministry is not as fruitful as you would like it to be? Strive for more wisdom by understanding God's energy in your life. Knowing your starting point is the precondition for taking the right steps.

SIX BASIC COLOR BLENDS

But how can you find out what your starting point is? On the following pages, I would like to give you six biblical examples, each of them representing one of six possible scenarios:

1. Strong in wisdom—weak in power and commitment
2. Strong in commitment—weak in power and wisdom
3. Strong in power—weak in commitment and wisdom
4. Strong in commitment and wisdom—weak in power
5. Strong in power and commitment—weak in wisdom
6. Strong in wisdom and power—weak in commitment

HOW GOD DEALS WITH IMPERFECT PEOPLE

When I have studied biblical examples of this kind, my attention has been drawn to the way God deals with imperfect people. He doesn't usually start by rebuking their weak points, but rather acknowledges the areas in which they are already strong. Translated into the terms of our three-colored diagram, he starts by appreciating the value of their most dominant color(s). And then—sometimes very gently, sometimes quite drastically—he opens their eyes to areas in which they are not yet strong and helps them enter those areas. Again, if we translate it into the terminology of our three-colored diagram, he helps them draw nearer to the center.

KNOWING YOUR STARTING POINT IS THE PRECONDITION FOR TAKING THE RIGHT STEPS.

DOES EVERYBODY NEED THE SAME THING?

In a way, all six of the biblical characters that I am about to describe needed exactly the same thing: to draw nearer to the center. However, the steps they had to take toward the center varied greatly according to their respective starting points. So we could say that each of these people needed *something very different* in order to finally reach the same destination.

If God deals with people in this way, then take the following pages as an invitation to discover the areas in which you are already strong, as well as those in which you need to grow.

STARTING POINT 1: THOMAS

CHAPTER 1: FOUNDATIONS

The Apostle Thomas ("Doubting Thomas") is an excellent illustration of what I would like to call the "skeptical believer" (see diagram to the right). Let's first have a look at his strong point which was, without a doubt, his critical, questioning mindset that strove to get to the heart of a matter. We should remember that one of Jesus' pivotal affirmations—"I am the way and the truth and the life. No one comes to the Father except through me"— had been provoked by Thomas' penetrating questions (John 14:5–6). If people like Thomas did not bother us with their sometimes uncomfortable questions, Christianity would very likely crawl down the road of progress.

WHILE THE SKEPTICAL BELIEVER IS STRONG IN WISDOM, HIS OR HER PRIMARY NEED IS FOR GROWTH IN BOTH POWER AND COMMITMENT.

We need people like Thomas in our churches, people who are simply not willing to take things for granted. They want to know reasons. They want to see proofs. None of us should criticize them for this, even if it might disturb the peace of the majority at times. Rather, all of us would be well-advised to learn from their perspective.

THOMAS' DEFICIENCIES

However, the New Testament indicates that Thomas' strength was also his weakness. In my experience, people with this degree of analytical thinking often fall short in the other two areas. As excellent as they may be in reflecting and questioning, commitment and power are not their strong points. They are often not present when decisive things happen, and

EXAMPLE: GORDON FROM GREAT BRITAIN

Gordon is a young Anglican priest who refuses to be put in any theological pigeonhole, yet (his protests not withstanding!) he probably has a certain tendency toward the **"liberal" wing** of his church. Without a doubt, Gordon is a spiritual man with **profound insight** not only into the Word of God, but also into its practical implications for church life. His lectures usually offer brilliant **analyses of Christianity**, and they frequently point out "blind spots" characteristic of different Christian groups. Hardly anything seems to be good enough for his **sophisticated standards**. For instance, his criticism of certain evangelistic methods is often justified, and both his evangelical and charismatic friends (and opponents) would benefit from paying closer attention to his words. However, it is characteristic that Gordon only rarely suggests positive ways to improve the practices he criticizes. Furthermore, whenever evangelism does take place (red segment), he is usually **conspicuously absent**.

His criticisms would carry much more weight if he were actually part of the game. If he would admit the limitations of a **purely rational approach** and pay more attention to his heart (blue segment), he might even dare to leave his sometimes **lonely position**.

The starting point of a "skeptical believer" such as Thomas. Their strength lies in the green area (wisdom); their weaknesses, in both the blue (power) and the red areas (commitment).

consequently they miss the special empowerment that results. While we are not told why, it is noteworthy that Thomas was not present when Jesus appeared to his disciples after his resurrection (John 20:24). On this occasion, aside from showing himself to his followers, Jesus foreshadowed the empowering they would receive from the Holy Spirit (John 20:22). Thomas simply missed this important event.

HOW JESUS DEALT WITH THOMAS

It is characteristic of someone like Thomas to say, "Unless I see the nail marks in his hands and put my finger where the nails were, and put my hand into his side, I will not believe it" (John 20:25). Now comes the most remarkable part of the story. Jesus did not react by criticizing Thomas for his weaknesses ("Doubting Thomas! I command you to repent!"). No, Jesus reacted differently. He started by responding to Thomas' strength, by fulfilling his desire for proofs, and said, "Reach out your hand and put it into my side." Only then did he say, "Stop doubting and believe" (John 20:27). Thus he revealed to Thomas an area of growth that was still await-ing him: "Because you have seen me, you have believed; blessed are those who have not seen and yet have believed" (John 20:29).

STARTING POINT 2: MARTHA

The starting point of the controlling believer is the red area (see diagram to the right). Controlling Christians are usually not very receptive to teaching on spiritual gifts or wisdom. In their eyes, all of that is too theoretical. They want to get things done, and they are usually those on whom you can count.

A fine biblical example of this starting point is Martha. In Luke 10:38–42 we read that she opened her home to Jesus and, unlike her sister Mary, served him at the table. This is characteristic of people like her. Their strength is commitment. Without the unselfish dedication of the "Marthas" of this world, we would probably close most of our churches.

WHILE THE CONTROLLING BELIEVER IS STRONG IN COMMITMENT, HIS OR HER PRIMARY NEED IS FOR GROWTH IN BOTH POWER AND WISDOM.

MARTHA'S DEFICIENCIES

This attitude of service was Martha's great strength, and Jesus didn't criticize this characteristic at all. However, the episode quoted below demonstrates Martha's weak points quite clearly. "But Martha was distracted by all the preparations that had to be made. She came to him (Jesus) and asked, 'Lord, don't you care that my sister has left me to do the work by myself? Tell her to help me!'" (Luke 10:40). In other words, she tried to manipulate her sister Mary so that she would become as active as herself. Like so many people who share this starting point, Martha didn't have a well-developed sense of the right timing *(kairos)*, which would be a characteristic typical of a wise person (green segment).

EXAMPLE: MICHAEL FROM AUSTRALIA

I met Michael at a seminar on "The Threefold Art of Experiencing God." During a coffee break he approached me and said, "Christian, what you teach sounds quite nice, but at the same time it is very theoretical. If something needs to be done, **I just do it!** I don't believe that all these reflections on gifts and wisdom will really get us anywhere. If the participants of this seminar were simply challenged to greater commitment in ministry, rather than filling in questionnaires and reflecting on their starting points, we would have achieved a lot." Later on, I learned from his pastor that Michael actually practices what he preaches. Whenever something needs to be done, the **pastor can count on him**. At the same time, Michael tends to give church members who don't share his level of commitment a **guilty conscience**. If he is in charge of a ministry, he sometimes creates a negative atmosphere by **pushing** his fellow believers to work harder.

His ministry would be much more effective and at the same time he would experience greater joy, if he combined his **commitment to the Lord** both with times of personal spiritual renewal (blue segment) and with greater wisdom in dealing with fellow Christians (green segment).

The starting point of a "controlling believer" such as Martha. Their strength lies in the red area (commitment); their weaknesses, in both the blue (power) and the green areas (wisdom).

In John 12:3 we are told that, while Martha was serving at the table, Mary poured out a pint of expensive perfume on Jesus' feet, so that the house was "filled with the fragrance of the perfume." The actions of the two women are consistent with what we already know of them—Martha was busy serving; Mary was busy worshiping. The danger for Martha, of course, was that in all her activity she might miss occasions of spiritual anointing (blue segment).

HOW JESUS DEALT WITH MARTHA

Jesus' response to Martha started with an acknowledgment of her unselfish commitment: "Martha, Martha, you are worried and upset about many things" (Luke 10:41). Without a doubt, Jesus appreciated this kind of ministry, as we can see by his reaction to other committed people. However, after he had said this, he added, "But only one thing is needed. Mary has chosen what is better, and it will not be taken away from her" (Luke 10:42). With these words, Jesus didn't disregard Martha's service, but by defending Mary's position he helped Martha discover an area in which she needed to grow.

CHAPTER 1:
FOUNDATIONS

STARTING POINT 3: MARY

I f Martha serves as an illustration of the controlling believer (who is most comfortable in the red segment), her sister, Mary, is the opposite. For people like Mary, only the blue segment matters (see diagram to the right). No wonder they had difficulties with each other!

Whereas we read in John's record of this story that Mary poured a whole pint of pure nard on Jesus' feet and wiped them with her hair (John 12:3), in Luke's narration, it is stressed that while Martha was serving, Mary simply "sat at the Lord's feet listening to what he said" (Luke 10:39). Both behaviors fit well with people like Mary. They have a strongly developed sensitivity to the spiritual dimension (blue segment). They can drop everything and throw caution to the wind. They can become excessive. It's understandable that Judas criticized Mary for this: "Why wasn't this perfume sold and the money given to the poor? It was worth a year's wages" (John 12:5). People like Mary don't care if they are confronted with such criticisms. They are driven by the inner conviction that they are spiritually correct. I understand why some people feel like they're going to go crazy when they have to deal with such people. While others are active, worried, and concerned, they just sit there "wasting" time and money! But this is exactly their strength.

> WHILE THE SPIRITUALIZING BELIEVER IS STRONG IN POWER, HIS OR HER PRIMARY NEED IS FOR GROWTH IN BOTH WISDOM AND COMMITMENT.

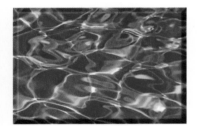

MARY'S DEFICIENCIES

It is somewhat difficult to criticize Mary's behavior, since Jesus clearly justified it. What, then, is the problem with "the spir-

EXAMPLE: LUCÍA FROM ARGENTINA

I've met Lucía at two different conferences. Both times she was involved in a powerful **ministry of intercession**, and I suspect that most of the participants could sense the difference it made when a meeting was upheld by **prayer warriors** like her. At the same time, Lucía gave some of the other co-workers the impression that they were "less spiritual" than herself, even if she never intended to communicate this. "Christian, **the only thing that we can do for church development is pray**," she told me time and again. And I always replied, "Lucía, your prayer ministry is wonderful. But, according to God's will, prayer is definitely not the only thing that we can and should do." Despite my words, I had the impression that while listening to me she was really thinking, "As convincing as it might sound, what Christian is teaching about church development is **not what really matters**."

To avoid misunderstanding, I must affirm that Lucía is a great woman and her ministry is **powerfully used by God**. I would not suggest that she withdraw one inch from her prayer ministry—quite the contrary! However, instead of presenting prayer (blue segment) as an alternative to both the "green" and the "red" dimensions, I would suggest that it is important for her to appreciate the spiritual relevance of all three dimensions of ministry.

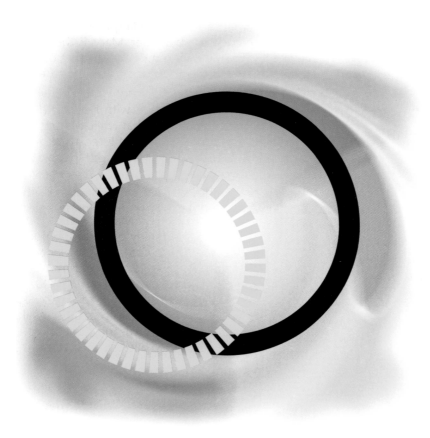

The starting point of a "spiritualizing believer" such as Mary. Their strength lies in the blue area (power); their weaknesses, in both the red (commitment) and the green areas (wisdom).

itualizing believer"? There is nothing wrong with Mary's behavior in this story; the specific situation clearly warranted it. However, there is a problem when spiritualizing believers make this sort of behavior a general pattern in their lives. They are *always* among those who sit around absorbing "spiritual things," while leaving the practical implications of ministry (red segment), together with all reflection and planning (green segment), to others.

How Jesus dealt with Mary

We shouldn't forget that Judas' criticism of Mary was not all wrong. When Jesus heard it, he first of all acknowledged the positive aspects of Mary's apparently extreme position. "It was intended that she should save this perfume for the day of my burial," he said, clearly foreshadowing the unique event that was to come (John 12:7). But then he went on to say, "You will always have the poor among you, but you will not always have me" (John 12:8). In other words, the time will come when you can—and should!—care for the poor again. Obviously, we cannot make Mary's behavior in this specific situation a general pattern for ministry!

STARTING POINT 4:
MOSES

Moses serves as a terrific illustration of what I have labeled the "burned-out believer" (see diagram to the right). Wisdom was certainly not his weakness. Acts 7:22 tells us that he had been "educated in all the wisdom of the Egyptians," and we can find traces of this throughout the whole Bible. Similarly, commitment was not an area of weakness for him. Anyone studying Moses' life will be amazed by his deep level of dedication.

WHILE THE BURNED-OUT BELIEVER IS STRONG IN BOTH WISDOM AND COMMITMENT, HIS OR HER PRIMARY NEED IS FOR GROWTH IN POWER.

MOSES' DEFICIENCY

Nevertheless, in the Bible we find a number of instances indicating that Moses lacked power in different ways. I would like to cite three of these episodes because they reveal to us the wonderful way in which God dealt with this (admitted!) lack of power in Moses' life.

The first episode is Moses' call to a challenging task. He was supposed to go to Pharaoh and lead God's people into liberty. Moses' reaction to this calling was negative. He didn't believe he had the strength for this task. "O Lord, I have never been eloquent," he said. "I am slow of speech and tongue" (Exodus 4:10). How did God react to this lack of power? He sent Moses' brother, Aaron, to speak to Pharaoh on Moses' behalf. The second episode illustrating Moses' lack of strength is the battle of the Israelites against the Amalekites. In Exodus 17:10–13 we read, "Moses, Aaron and Hur went to the top of the hill. As long as Moses held up his

EXAMPLE: CATHY FROM THE UNITED STATES

Without a doubt, Cathy is one of the **most devoted Christians** I've ever met. The number of responsibilities she carries, both in her local church and beyond, is incredible. On top of this, Cathy is an extremely **educated woman**, so each of her words carries a lot of weight. I enjoy interacting with her, and I am always astonished by what one person can **achieve for the kingdom of God**. One time I asked her, "Cathy, don't you feel burned out right now?" Without hesitation, she answered affirmatively and added, "But isn't that our job description as Christians, **burning out for the Lord**?" Cathy's problem isn't that she feels burned out at times—a lot of dedicated Christian workers go through those seasons—but that she makes the **"burn-out syndrome" her lifestyle**.

I have no doubt that, in the long run, she would be even more effective in ministry if she took more time to experience that in God's eyes she, as a person, is **more important than all of her dedicated ministry**. It would also be beneficial for her to accept the fact that she doesn't have to **do everything herself**. There are so many Christians like Cathy who could achieve much more if only they were empowered for ministry (blue segment).

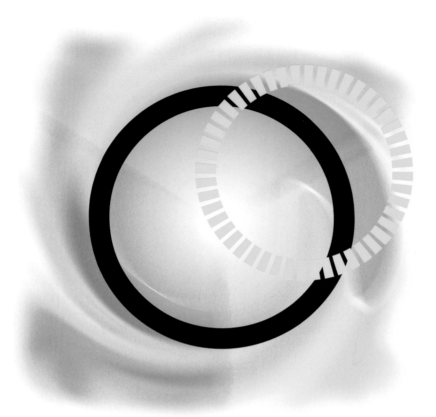

The starting point of a "burned-out believer" such as Moses. Their strengths lie both in the green (wisdom) and the red areas (commitment); their weakness, in the blue area (power).

hands, the Israelites were winning, but whenever he lowered his hands, the Amalekites were winning. When Moses' hands grew tired, they took a stone and put it under him and he sat on it. Aaron and Hur held his hands up—one on one side, one on the other—so that his hands remained steady till sunset. So Joshua overcame the Amalekite army." The third episode is Jethro's visit to Moses, as recorded in Exodus 18. There we learn that Moses served his people as judge from morning till evening. Jethro told him, "You and these people who come to you will only wear yourselves out. The work is too heavy for you; you cannot handle it alone" (Exodus 18:18). He advised Moses to select capable people who would serve as judges over thousands, hundreds, fifties and tens, leaving only the difficult cases for Moses.

How God dealt with Moses

Again, it is noteworthy to see how God dealt with Moses' obvious lack of power. In all three cases, he sent people who were strong where Moses was weak. In the first episode, this was Aaron; in the second, Aaron and Hur; and in the third, his father-in-law Jethro. In all three cases, the success of these "joint ventures" was remarkable.

CHAPTER 1:
FOUNDATIONS

STARTING POINT 5: PETER

I have chosen Peter as a biblical illustration of the "fanatical believer" (see diagram to the right). People like him are not lacking commitment. They are ready to take risks for the Lord. Look at the episode that some Bibles have subtitled "Sinking Peter." We should note that Peter was the only disciple who dared to leave the boat to meet Jesus, who was walking on the water. "Lord, if it's you," he said, "tell me to come to you on the water" (Matthew 14:28). It is true that later he lost his faith and sank, but his risk-taking attitude remains remarkable. Thus, "Daring Peter" or "Risk-taking Peter" would be a far better subtitle for this story.

> WHILE THE FANATICAL BELIEVER IS STRONG IN BOTH POWER AND COMMITMENT, HIS OR HER PRIMARY NEED IS FOR GROWTH IN WISDOM.

The same holds true for the famous episode which speaks about how Peter disowned Jesus (Matthew 26:69–75). Again, we shouldn't forget that he was probably the only disciple who followed Jesus right into the courtyard, whereas all the others disappeared. What courage, and what love for the Lord!

When we consider the "blue segment," we make similar discoveries. In the entire book of Acts, hardly another person's ministry is accompanied by as many supernatural signs and wonders as Peter's. He was clearly a man of both power and commitment.

PETER'S DEFICIENCY

Wisdom (the green segment) doesn't seem to be one of Peter's strengths. When Jesus was arrested, it was Peter who

EXAMPLE: SULASTRI FROM INDONESIA

I have learned so much from Sulastri in terms of both **spiritual power and commitment to the Lord** that at first I thought her life would be an almost perfect representation of what Christian ministry should be. I could clearly sense that she didn't minister in her own power, but in the power of the Holy Spirit, and that she was simply **obedient** in doing this. But then I learned that in many instances Sulastri, with all her power and commitment, **lacked sensitivity toward others** and quite often didn't demonstrate a well-developed sense of the right timing. Thus, she sometimes acted like **a bull in a china shop**. She had difficulty understanding that in spite of all of her wonderful activities, she could do a lot of harm. Her strength really wasn't sitting down and reflecting on what she, or other Christians, should do in order to achieve a specific goal. The motto of her life was simply, **"Pray and obey."**

But it is precisely this kind of self-reflection, together with the humility to learn from others (who might not even share her level of power and commitment), that are crucial for her to make further progress in her spiritual life. It is in the "green segment" of our diagram where she could find the key to even more effective ministry. Sulastri has so much to teach all of us, if only she could do it **more wisely**.

The starting point of a "fanatical believer" such as Peter. Their strengths lie both in the blue (power) and the red areas (commitment); their weakness, in the green area (wisdom).

tried to defend him by cutting off the right ear of the high priest's servant (John 18:10–11). Peter's motto, like many others who share his starting point, appears to be, "It's better to do something wrong than to do nothing at all!" And thus it happens that a servant loses his ear. People like Peter have difficulty noticing how much harm their powerful commitment causes if it is not tempered by wisdom.

How Jesus dealt with Peter

We all know the end of the story. Jesus told Peter, "No more of this!" Then he touched the servant's ear and healed him (Luke 22:51). He saw the lack of wisdom, the lack of balance and the lack of diplomacy in Peter's life, and yet Jesus told him, "On this rock I will build my church" (Matthew 16:18).

It is remarkable that Peter's obedience and spiritual power seemed to be more important than his deficiency in wisdom for the leadership position Jesus had in mind. Jesus repeatedly gave Peter another chance, including opportunities to grow in wisdom. And in the book of Acts we find some hints that Peter made progress.

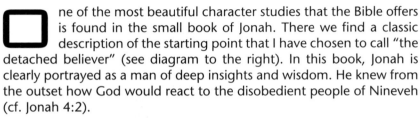

CHAPTER 1:
FOUNDATIONS

STARTING POINT 6: JONAH

O ne of the most beautiful character studies that the Bible offers is found in the small book of Jonah. There we find a classic description of the starting point that I have chosen to call "the detached believer" (see diagram to the right). In this book, Jonah is clearly portrayed as a man of deep insights and wisdom. He knew from the outset how God would react to the disobedient people of Nineveh (cf. Jonah 4:2).

WHILE THE DETACHED BELIEVER IS STRONG IN BOTH POWER AND WISDOM, HIS OR HER PRIMARY NEED IS FOR GROWTH IN COMMITMENT.

Throughout this book, we also learn of Jonah's power. Whatever he did bore fruit. Having heard Jonah's testimony, and especially after having thrown him overboard, the men on the ship "greatly feared the Lord, and they offered a sacrifice to the Lord and made vows to him" (Jonah 1:16). This was a direct consequence of Jonah's ministry!

When he finally preached God's message to the people of Nineveh, the result was remarkable. The people of Nineveh repented (Jonah 3:5). Now, it is true that Jonah didn't like this outcome very much (Jonah 4:1), but it was the result of his extremely powerful ministry.

JONAH'S DEFICIENCY

Jonah's weak point isn't difficult to identify. He lacked commitment. He was not willing to do what the Lord commanded him to do. He fled from God, and he fled from fulfilling God's mission. Or better said, he *tried* to flee, since the Lord didn't let him get away with it!

EXAMPLE: NDOZE FROM NAMIBIA

I know Ndoze only through e-mail, but in almost all of his correspondence I find hints that he is a person full of both **spiritual power and wisdom**. But when it comes to follow-through, especially in the face of difficulties, there is still a lot for him to learn. I got in contact with Ndoze when he invited me to a conference in Africa. Even through his written words, I could sense that he was a man of spiritual power. He attached to his e-mail a paper describing the long-term strategy behind this conference, and I must admit that I have seldom read such an excellent, **well-thought-out** paper. All of it looked so marvelous that I was truly disappointed that I was unable to accept his invitation. Later on, however, I heard that the conference never took place, as is the case with so many things that Ndoze plans. Of course, he usually has a good explanation when this occurs, but it is remarkable how often this sort of thing happens in his life.

In Ndoze's own surroundings, his fellow Christians view him rather critically. Yes, they can sense that he is a **visionary man of God** and that he has many **valuable insights** to offer, but they regard him as **too unreliable** to work with. If Ndoze could simply improve his level of self-discipline (red segment), both his power and wisdom would be released for the benefit of the body of Christ.

The starting point of a "detached believer" such as Jonah. Their strengths lie both in the blue (power) and the green areas (wisdom); their weakness, in the red area (commitment).

HOW GOD DEALT WITH JONAH

Anyone who wants to learn how God deals with disobedient people should carefully study the book of Jonah. God acted both lovingly—and drastically. He allowed Jonah to be thrown into the sea—and provided a fish to swallow him. He let Jonah "digest" matters for three days—and commanded the fish to vomit him back onto the land. Later when the sun was burning on Jonah's head, God provided a vine to give him shade—and sent a worm that chewed the vine so that it withered. All of this sounds almost brutal. Why did God treat Jonah this way? Because of Jonah's starting point. He was a man of extraordinary power and wisdom. How do you teach obedience to a person who knows the will of God and who has success in his or her ministry? God probably wouldn't have treated a person from another starting point in the same way, but toward a man like Jonah, this treatment was quite loving.

Detached believers, watch out! The Lord might need to educate you in the school of hard knocks. Do you want to move nearer to the center? *Your* way to this destination is "obedience."

CHAPTER 1:
FOUNDATIONS

YOUR PERSONAL CHARACTER COMPASS

After studying the six starting points, you probably already sense which of the examples resembles your own situation. The next four pages will help you collect further information about where your own starting point is with regard to the three dimensions of ministry. Once you have identified your personal starting point, the next steps you should take to experience further spiritual growth should be quite evident. Whatever your starting point may be, the goal of your journey is always to draw nearer to the center; in other words, closer to the triune God.

THE CHARACTER COMPASS AS AN ETEST

In order to identify your personal starting point, we recommend you take the following test as an online eTest rather than filling in the printed tables. You can access the eTest version at *3colorworld.org/compass*. Doing the eTest has the following advantages:

WHATEVER YOUR STARTING POSITION MIGHT BE, THE GOAL OF YOUR JOURNEY IS ALWAYS TO DRAW NEARER TO THE CENTER.

1. The procedure is quicker and simpler than evaluating the test manually.

2. As a result, you will get a detailed report celebrating your starting point and suggesting steps for further growth.

3. The eTest is free.

4. When working with a group, you can easily invite others and produce a group profile.

THE PRINT-VERSION OF THE TEST

However, if you prefer to use the printed version, you can follow the five steps that you will find in the yellow boxes at the bottom of the next four pages. Pages 42–44 give you suggestions as to how these results might help you in working through the remaining chapters of this book. Enjoy the exercise!

STEP 1:

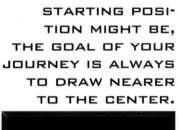

Look at the table on page 39. There you will find ten rows, each containing three adjectives. Indicate in each row which of these adjectives describes you *best* (**2**), *second best* (**1**), or *least* (**0**).

When doing this exercise, think primarily of your experiences throughout the past few months.

	Column A		Column B		Column C	
1	energetic	0	knowledgable	1	active	2
2	passionate	1	rational	2	analytical	~~0~~
3	reluctant	~~1~~	reserved	2	demanding	0
4	spontaneous	0	reflective	1	stable	2
5	emotional	2	rigid	~~1~~	ultra-careful	0
6	cheerful	0	open-minded	1	devoted	2
7	self-denying	~~0~~	enlightened	1	dutiful	2
8	Spirit-led	2	objective	0	reliable	1
9	impulsive	1	sophisticated	2	unstable	~~0~~
10	enthusiastic	1	excitable	~~0~~	disciplined	2
	Total A	7 ~~8~~	**Total B**	10 ~~11~~	**Total C**	11 ~~13~~

Please mark in each of the ten rows:

2
= word that describes me best

1
= word that describes me second best

0
= word that describes me least

STEP 2:

Cross out the values of the following boxes: **A 3, A 7, B 5, B 10, C 2** and **C 9**.

STEP 3:

Now add up the remaining figures in each of the three columns and fill in the results beside *Total A, Total B,* and *Total C.* Then turn to the next page.

WHERE ARE YOU AT THE MOMENT?

*Place an X on each of the three dotted lines at the location corresponding to the numbers you have calculated for **Total A, Total B,** and **Total C.***

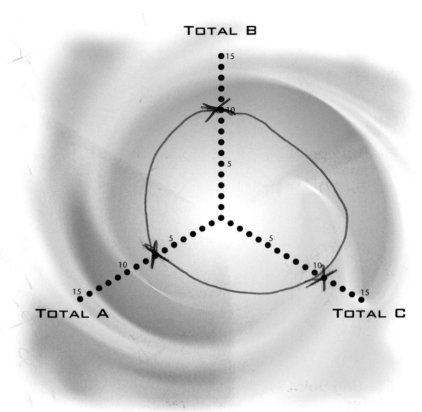

TOTAL B

TOTAL A

TOTAL C

STEP 4:

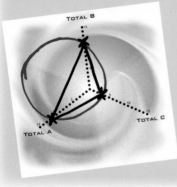

In the diagram above ("Where are you at the moment?") place an X on each of the three dotted lines at the location corresponding to the numbers you have calculated for *Total A, Total B,* and *Total C.* Connect these three points to make a triangle.

Then draw a circle around the triangle (which should intersect the three dots), so that your personal diagram looks similar to one of the six starting points on page 41.

WHAT DOES YOUR CHARACTER COMPASS LOOK LIKE?

☐ **Starting point 1:**
Thomas
(see pp. 26–27)

☒ **Starting point 2:**
Martha
(see pp. 28–29)

☐ **Starting point 3:**
Mary
(see pp. 30–31)

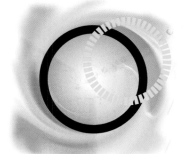

☒ **Starting point 4:**
Moses
(see pp. 32–33)

☐ **Starting point 5:**
Peter
(see pp. 34–35)

☐ **Starting point 6:**
Jonah
(see pp. 36–37)

STEP 5:

☐ Starting point 6:
Jonah
(see pp. 36–37)

Compare your own *Character Compass* with the representations of the six starting points above. Which does it most resemble?

Mark that diagram with an X. If your own diagram is a mixture of two starting points, mark both options.

Review the descriptions of your own starting point(s) on the pages indicated.

Then turn to page 42.

THE NEXT STEPS

Are you surprised by the results? Or do they just confirm what you have anticipated from the beginning? When interpreting your personal *Character Compass*, you should take the following points into consideration:

• The diagram merely serves to highlight your tendencies. It does *not* give an answer to the question of how strong or weak these tendencies are.

• It might be that you are among the 4.6 percent who have a relatively "balanced" diagram with basically the same score in all three areas. If this is the case, you shouldn't conclude that you have already reached your goal; this just tells you that there is no dominant problem area. In other words: Growth in each and every dimension would be beneficial for you.

THE CHARACTER COMPASS SHOWS YOU THE DIRECTION IN WHICH YOU NEED TO TAKE STEPS TO BECOME MORE EFFECTIVE IN THE KINGDOM OF GOD.

• The diagram represents your tendencies as they are *right now*. If you were to repeat the test some months or years from now, you might get different results. If your circumstances have changed or you have matured spiritually, you will see the effects.

• When you work with other books in this series, you might identify different "colors" in different areas. For example, in the book *The 3 Colors of Love* you might identify primarily "green" tendencies, whereas in the book *The 3 Colors of Your Spirituality* your tendencies might be "red." Results like these are normal. Life is too complex to expect a uniform pattern.

• The same could be true when you identify your spiritual gifts later on. It might be that your gifts lie primarily in the "red" area, while you have identified "commitment" as your primary color deficiency. Don't expect that you will only reflect one color in every single aspect of your life.

THREE KEY QUESTIONS

On the next two pages, I give some practical suggestions on how the rest of this book can benefit people from each of the six starting points. Before moving to this section, you should take some time to answer the following questions:

1. Where am I at the moment? Which biblical or contemporary examples do I resemble most? (This will, at the same time, answer the question of which area has the greatest "color deficiency" in your life.)

2. What can I do in order to grow in the area of my "color deficiency"?

3. How can I better invest my strengths into the development of my church? (Remember that you have not only identified "color deficiencies," but also remarkable strengths in one or even in two of the three areas.)

NEXT STEPS FOR "THOMAS"

If you belong to this category, the process of mentally *relating* the gifts that you will identify (blue segment) to concrete tasks (red segment) will probably not be too difficult for you (for representatives of other starting points this can be an extremely difficult task, and you could help them in this endeavor). However, you must relate your gifts to real tasks and not just hold the right theories on the subject. You have much more spiritual potential than you are using right now. Your church could profit so much from your wisdom.

NEXT STEPS FOR "MARTHA"

You are already very committed in your ministry, but you often lack power. Simply discovering your spiritual gifts (blue segment) and reorganizing your existing ministry involvements in the light of your new discoveries (green segment) could result in a spiritual breakthrough for you. Maybe you need to discontinue your involvement in some ministries and substitute them with others. Your level of commitment will be of tremendous help in this process. You may also find that you are filled with new enthusiasm for your remaining ministries.

NEXT STEPS FOR "MARY"

There is much more power in you than is already being released for the benefit of others. When you enter the gift discovery process, you will probably identify many gifts of which you are already aware. Your problem may not be so much that you don't use them, but that you are far too reluctant to relate your wonderful gifts to concrete tasks (red segment) within your church in a strategic way (green segment). This would empower you even more. Put it to the test!

NEXT STEPS FOR "MOSES"

You place a high value on commitment, and your sense of duty seems to be highly developed. Moreover, you are capable of reflecting on your own and on others' ministry involvements. People in leadership positions often share your starting point. What you may tend to neglect are your emotions. Focusing your attention on that area could make you stronger. It is highly probable that the simple act of gift discovery will have a more dramatic result in your life than it will have for representatives of any of the other five starting points.

NEXT STEPS FOR "PETER"

You are quite active in ministry, but not everything that you do is very well thought through. Probably even the approach of this book will be "too theoretical" for you. Trust me; that is not true! The "theory" of this book could be especially beneficial for you. When studying this book, pay special attention to those areas that you don't like that much. Most likely you will find the key to further spiritual growth right there. Don't regard certain concepts as "unspiritual" just because they might be unfamiliar to you.

NEXT STEPS FOR "JONAH"

It is probably not a strange exercise for you to identify your spiritual gifts (blue segment) with the help of a scientific online test (green segment). In contrast to other Christians, you probably enjoy this kind of exercise. Your area of focus should be commitment. This doesn't necessarily mean that you aren't active; maybe you are. But if you are, your activities are almost exclusively determined by yourself, not so much by the expectations and needs of others. Commitment to other people will be the key to *your* success.

GOD LOVES TO USE IMPERFECT PEOPLE

This chapter has dealt primarily with "color deficiencies"—in other words, with weaknesses. I believe that this study has been necessary in order to give you an indication of your starting point. On the other hand, this procedure also carries a potential danger. It could be frustrating to focus exclusively on your weak points.

You should never forget that God has constantly used people with clearly visible "color deficiencies" to achieve his goals. He used a Peter without wisdom to give leadership to the church. He used a Moses without power to set his people free. He used a Jonah without commitment to save the people of Nineveh.

In my opinion, the real lesson that we can learn from studying the six starting points is that God uses imperfect people to achieve his perfect goals. He clearly wants each of us to grow in faith and in maturity, no doubt about it! But he doesn't wait until we are perfect before using us.

If you keep this message in mind, your work on your specific "color deficiency" can be a joyful and fulfilling undertaking. In the chapter *Practical Steps* on page 73 you will find concrete suggestions on how the results of your *Character Compass* can be combined with the result of the *Three-Color Gift Test*.

WHAT YOU SHOULD KNOW ABOUT SPIRITUAL GIFTS

In the past few years, there has been an increasing interest among believers all over the world in discovering their spiritual gifts. What's the reason for this remarkable development? It seems to me, the best explanation might simply be that this is God's plan for our generation. Apparently, God has placed the theme of "spiritual gifts" on today's agenda. It is his desire that we acquaint ourselves with the gifts that he has already given to us.

CHAPTER 2:
UNDERSTANDING
GIFTS

EVERYBODY IS GIFTED

Asurvey conducted by our institute among 1,200 Christians yielded a shocking result: 80 percent of those surveyed had no idea what their spiritual gifts might be. Only 20 percent indicated that they knew what their spiritual gifts were and used them.

IF YOU DON'T KNOW WHAT YOUR GIFTS ARE, IT IS SIMPLY BECAUSE YOU HAVE NEVER DISCOVERED THEM.

How can we explain this? The New Testament teaches us that each member of the body of Christ has received at least one spiritual gift. We can assume that there are some Christians who do, in fact, use their gifts; but when asked in a survey, they have difficulty affirming this. In recent years I have met many people who don't believe they have any spiritual gifts, and yet it is evident to others that they are using their gifts for the glory of God. Nevertheless, if 80 percent of all Christians are uncertain about their gifts, this reveals a critical spiritual situation. Apparently, in the past we have failed to give this topic the attention that it deserves.

A WORKING DEFINITION

Just what do I mean when I refer to "spiritual gifts"? My experience over the past few years has been that the following definition is well-received by a wide variety of Christian groups:

A spiritual gift is a special ability that God gives, according to his grace, to each member of the body of Christ to be used for the development of the church.

Each element in this definition is important for the concept of spiritual gifts upon which this book is based:

- *A special ability:* Every person has a different gift mix. When you discover your gift(s), you can be sure that this places you in a minority. It is not to be expected that any one gift is possessed by the majority of people. Just as the human body has a variety of members and organs, so the body of Christ—the church—is comprised of a great variety of Christians, each of whom has his or her own special function (cf. Rom. 12:4–8; 1 Cor. 12:17–20). Which functions each member is to fulfill is determined, for the most part, by his or her spiritual gift(s).

- *God:* Throughout the world, Christians have differing concepts of spiritual gifts, which largely correspond to differing views of God (as we have seen in the first chapter). There are groups that only consider gifts that are not imparted by God through creation as "spiritual." For others, only the creation gifts are valid and the whole area of the supernatural is viewed skeptically. Others focus primarily, if not exclusively, on a gift's contribution to the Great Commission. All of them have good arguments for their respective positions. This book is based on a trinitarian approach. Whether we encounter the

Creator, Jesus, or the Holy Spirit, we always meet the same God, just in different ways. This has very practical consequences for our understanding of spiritual gifts. Whether we believe that gifts are imparted by the Creator, by Jesus, or by the Holy Spirit, in the end they are always imparted by God. We can be sure that we are using them according to God's will if we use them to his glory and for the benefit of others. For this reason, this book demonstrates how gifts can be discovered and used in all three areas.

- *According to his grace:* God doesn't give you spiritual gifts as a reward for your steadfast character or spiritual maturity. He imparts them according to his grace (cf. Rom. 12:6). Spiritual gifts are not to be confused with "the fruit of the Spirit" (cf. Gal. 5:22). I have met many individuals whom God abundantly blessed with spiritual gifts immediately after their conversion, and because they were so young in their faith, they used them quite immaturely. Spiritual gifts are by no means a reward for faithfulness. They are distributed according to God's plan.

- *Each member of the body of Christ:* Every Christian has at least one spiritual gift (1 Cor. 12: 7–11). If you are a Christian and don't know your gifts, it is not because God has not gifted you. It is exclusively due to the fact that you have not yet discovered them.

SPIRITUAL GIFTS ARE BY NO MEANS A REWARD FOR FAITHFULNESS. THEY ARE DISTRIBUTED ACCORDING TO GOD'S PLAN.

- *For the development of the church:* All of the major statements in the New Testament relating to spiritual gifts are made in the context of the body of Christ and its growth (Rom. 12; 1 Cor. 12; Eph. 4). Spiritual gifts are not just for the growth of individual believers; their primary purpose is to benefit others (cf. 1 Cor. 14:2–5; Eph. 4:12; 1 Pet. 4:10). Anyone who withdraws from Christian fellowship cannot use his or her gifts as God intended. Any reflections upon spiritual gifts must occur in connection with church development. That is the main reason why I have combined both themes in this book. It's really just one theme; if we separate it, we inevitably run into problems.

YOUR THOUGHTS:

- *Do you know anyone whose whose use of spiritual gifts you admire? Write down any names that come to your mind.*
- *Perhaps you have specific questions related to spiritual gifts which you would like to have answered while working through this book. There is value in writing down such questions at the very beginning of the process.*

GIFTS AND CALLING

M any Christians are moved by the question, "What might be God's calling for my life?" In speaking with them, I sometimes get the impression that they believe God enjoys calling us to tasks that in no way correspond to our gifting.

I recall visiting a young German who was toying with the idea that God might be calling him to serve in Africa as an evangelist. I asked him if he had the gift of evangelism and the gift of missionary, since both of them would be very important for fulfilling this challenging task. He told me that he had never thought about it, and then added, "If God really is calling me to such a ministry, he doesn't care about my gifting."

SOME PEOPLE ARE OF THE OPINION THAT GOD ENJOYS CALLING US TO TASKS THAT IN NO WAY CORRESPOND TO OUR GIFTING.

I have no idea who taught him this concept, but when I told him that I thought this was sheer nonsense, he became angry with me. It was apparent that the way he was brought up as a Christian caused him to believe that "calling" and "gifting" are almost contradictory concepts; so he perceived my words as an attack on his Christian beliefs.

THE SPIRITUAL SIGNIFICANCE OF GIFT DISCOVERY

God doesn't call you to a task for which he hasn't endowed you with the corresponding gifts. Said another way, if you discover your gifts, you know to which areas of ministry God is calling you. If you discover that you have a particular gift, but don't use it, you can be quite sure that you aren't living up to your calling. Would you like to find out if God has called you to a leadership position? Test whether you have the gift of leadership. There are other criteria for leaders as well, but without the corresponding gift you will have difficulty in any leadership role. Would you like to know whether God has called you to a counseling ministry? Then find out whether you have the corresponding gift. The discovery of spiritual gifts is a very important step toward determining your calling.

YOUR THOUGHTS:

• *Are there specific tasks to which you are certain God has called you? What are they?*

• *To what extent do these tasks correspond to your spiritual gifts?*

WHAT'S YOUR GIFT MIX?

I know a Christian who has the gifts of evangelism, prophecy, and mercy. Another one has the gifts of service and hospitality. Still another one has the gifts of healing, teaching, service, and mercy. A fourth one has the gift of counseling. It's wonderful to see how God has blessed different people with such a variety of gifts. None of us has reason to be proud of our individual gift mix, since each one of us depends upon the gifts of others to complement our own gifts (cf. Rom. 12:3; 1 Cor. 12:21–23). At the same time, there is no reason to be jealous of the gifts of others as God will only hold us accountable for the gifts he actually has given to us (cf. 1 Peter 4:10; Matt. 25:14–30).

AN IMPORTANT STEP: FIND OUT WHICH GIFTS YOU DON'T HAVE

Each person has his or her unique gift mix. As I set out to discover my own spiritual gifts, I first found out which gifts God had *not* given me—and this list was rather long. Included in this list were gifts such as deliverance, mercy, interpretation of tongues, evangelism, hospitality, and many more.

Initially I was somewhat disappointed that there were so many gifts I didn't have, but the more I thought about it, the more apparent it became to me that each time I discover a gift that I don't have is a cause to celebrate. Through this discovery God has shown me that I shouldn't make these areas a focus for my ministry.

EACH TIME I DISCOVER A GIFT THAT I *DON'T* HAVE IS A CAUSE TO CELEBRATE.

HOW CHRISTIANS COMPLEMENT EACH OTHER

Through this process I discovered that God has given me two primary gifts: the gift of teaching and the gift of faith. While I say this with confidence, I am very much aware of how dependent I am upon the gifts of other Christians—and how dependent they are upon mine, as well. For example, one of our former employees volunteered for a number of ministries, including tasks that most Christians would regard as rather boring. When I first observed her level of commitment, I almost felt guilty. Then we discovered that she had the gift of helps and realized that by using her time and energy to aid our ministry, she was simply fulfilling her calling. By integrating her gifts into our ministry, I was able to offer her the opportunity to be a part of projects that she never could have done alone. And that was the best thing that could have happened—for her as well as for me.

YOUR THOUGHTS:

• *When you consider the list of gifts on page 89, are there certain gifts that you are relatively certain that you do not have? Write them down.*

CHAPTER 2:
UNDERSTANDING
GIFTS

MISTAKES ARE ALLOWED

When I am invited to conduct a seminar at a Christian conference, I am able, with a clear conscience, to tell the participants that God has given me the gift of teaching, and that in the next few hours they will experience how God uses this gift in my life.

This doesn't mean, however, that I see myself as being an exceptionally gifted teacher. I know some Christians to whom God has given the same gift to a far higher degree. However, that does not change the fact that God has gifted me in this area and that he expects me to exercise this gift. I am also aware that there are times when I am inadequately prepared, impatient, lack focus, or simply have had too little sleep. Just because I am practicing my spiritual gifts doesn't mean that everything will turn out perfectly.

It is important to understand that the same gift can occur in different *variations* and to different *degrees*.

EXERCISING YOUR SPIRITUAL GIFTS DOES NOT MEAN THAT EVERYTHING WILL TURN OUT PERFECTLY.

DIFFERENT VARIATIONS OF GIFTS

For example, one person may be particularly gifted in applying the gift of evangelism in sermons; another person may use the same gift in personal conversation; yet another one might be most effective in utilizing this gift in writing evangelistic tracts; and a fourth person may demonstrate the gift of evangelism in working with children. These are all different variations of the same gift. It's imperative that we free ourselves from the concept that there is only one way to apply our gifts. Not everyone with the gift of evangelism has to use it in the same way Billy Graham does.

DIFFERENT DEGREES OF GIFTEDNESS

Even if two Christians have the same variation of a gift, they may have it to very different degrees. I have met literally thousands of Christians whom God has blessed with the gift of evangelism, and a lot of them are exercising it in a very unspectacular but effective way. Many of them, however, are so fixed on the "Billy Graham model" that they are not able to perceive their own divine gifting. Comparing oneself with others who have the same gift to a far greater degree can actually turn out to be more frustrating than inspiring.

YOUR THOUGHTS:

• *Choose one gift, from the list on page 89, which you think you have. (If you are uncertain, simply choose a gift that you would like to have.) Write down some possible variations of this gift.*

IS YOUR GIFTING PERMANENT?

Once you have discovered a spiritual gift, you can assume that it is to be used for your entire lifetime. There are exceptions to this rule. However, when it comes to general principles for our lives, it is far more productive to concentrate on the rules rather than on the exceptions.

SINCE GIFTS ARE INTENDED FOR LIFELONG USE, WE CAN PLAN OUR LIVES ACCORDINGLY.

Some people believe that spiritual gifts are given according to the need of the moment and that they then disappear just as quickly. I believe that this phenomenon does exist—God commissions certain persons to perform certain tasks according to a specific need and empowers them just for that very moment. This does happen and all of us should be open to it, but it should not be confused with a spiritual gift. Spiritual gifts are intended for permanent use.

PAUL AND THE GIFT OF MISSIONARY

When God gave Paul the gift of missionary, it was intended to be applied for the full extent of his lifetime. The apostle was able to build on this premise, plan his life, and carry out his ministry accordingly. When he left port for Greece, he never had any reason to doubt that he possessed the gift of missionary or that he might later discover, to his astonishment, that God had taken this gift from him some time during his travels.

THE IMAGE OF THE BODY

The New Testament repeatedly speaks of spiritual gifts in the context of the body of Christ. We can conclude that gifts do not appear completely unexpectedly and then disappear just as suddenly. How could a healthy body function like this? In God's creation, the hand need not fear that tomorrow morning it will be an ear, and that the following day it might wake up as a liver!

Since the Holy Spirit imparts his gifts to us for permanent use, we can plan our lives based on the discovery of our gifts and use them for the benefit of others and the development of the church.

YOUR THOUGHTS:

• *How do you react to the idea that the gifts you discover should be used throughout your life? Is this statement freeing for you, or more of a burden? Why?*

SPIRITUAL GIFTS AND UNIVERSAL RESPONSIBILITIES

Universal responsibilities apply to all Christians, regardless of whether or not they might be gifted in those areas. Every spiritual gift corresponds to a universal responsibility. The difference between these two categories is the following: The application of each spiritual gift cannot be expected from every person, but only from those who have the corresponding gift. Universal responsibilities, on the other hand, are to be practiced by all Christians.

PEOPLE WHO DON'T HAVE THE GIFT OF EVANGELISM ARE NOT EXCUSED FROM THE RESPONSIBILITY TO SHARE THEIR FAITH.

Not every Christian has the gift of evangelism, but all Christians have the responsibility of sharing their faith. It is simply one of their duties as a Christian. In order to tell others of your faith, you do not need to have the gift of evangelism.

Not every Christian has the gift of giving, but putting a portion of one's income at the Lord's disposal does apply to every Christian. You certainly don't need the gift of giving in order to tithe.

Not every Christian has the gift of faith, yet every Christian does have the universal responsibility of trusting Christ in all of life's dilemmas. In order to entrust your life to God, it is not necessary to have the distinct gift of faith.

The distinction between spiritual gifts and universal responsibilities is far more than just semantics. It can protect us from drifting astray in the following two ways:

THE DANGER OF "GIFT PROJECTION"

On the one hand, this distinction prevents us from expecting what can only be expected from those who have the corresponding spiritual gift. Chapter 4 of this book will address the danger which C. Peter Wagner refers to as "gift projection" (see page 87).

For example, Christians who have the gift of evangelism tend to expect of other Christians the same kind of evangelistic involvement that is normal for them—much to the detriment of the body of Christ. Such an expectation is neutralized when we distinguish between spiritual gifts and universal Christian responsibilities.

THE DANGER OF DISOBEDIENCE

At the same time, this distinction prevents the teaching of spiritual gifts to be used as a justification for a lack of commitment or even disobedience.

For example, even if you do not have the gift of evangelism, you are not excused from the responsibility of sharing your faith with others. This is one of the universal Christian responsibilities which can and should be practiced by each and every Christian.

YOUR THOUGHTS:

• *What are the universal responsibilities that relate to the different spiritual gifts? Record as many examples as possible in the left column (see the gift list on page 89) and write down the corresponding universal responsibilities in the right column.*

Spiritual gift

Evangelism

Giving

Mercy
Faith
Healing
Prophecy

_____

_____

_____

_____

_____

_____

_____

_____

_____

Universal responsibility

Personal testimony

Tithing

Missions
Encouragement
Praying for others
Guidance, Counseling

_____

_____

_____

_____

_____

_____

_____

_____

_____

JUST HOW MANY GIFTS ARE THERE ANYWAY?

Anyone who examines the three major gift lists in the New Testament (Romans 12; 1 Corinthians 12; Ephesians 4) will make an interesting discovery. Each of these lists differs considerably from the others. Apparently, none of them claims to be a complete list of all the possibilities which God has in store for his church. In writing to the Corinthians, Paul mentions certain gifts that are not included in his epistle to the Romans; and he highlights still others in his letter to the Ephesians.

This suggests a great diversity in the gifts God gives. It also implies that we shouldn't be dogmatic about the number of gifts there might be. Surely then, when it comes to spiritual gifts, the question of *how many* spiritual gifts there are is less important than *what they are for*. God gives them so that the church can fulfill specific tasks.

CAN GOD GIVE NEW GIFTS?

My personal opinion is that we should be open to the possibility that God may give us gifts today which are not even mentioned among the spiritual gifts in the Bible.

APPARENTLY, NONE OF THE NEW TESTAMENT GIFT LISTS CLAIMS TO BE COMPLETE.

For example, the New Testament nowhere speaks explicitly of the spiritual gift of prayer. Yet there can be no doubt that there are certain Christians whom God has blessed with a unique power in prayer. Anyone who joyfully prays two or three hours, day after day, and experiences extraordinary answers to prayer has most likely been endowed with a spiritual gift for prayer.

THE MOST IMPORTANT CRITERION

However, I must add that I am not dogmatic about this view. Whatever phrases we might use in order to describe our experiences—"natural abilities," "supernatural anointings," "charismatic occurrences," "motivational gifts," "inspirational gifts," "sign gifts," etc.—the point is that we always speak about gifts as tools from God that should be used for his glory and for the development of his church. In light of this challenge, discussions regarding terminology may not be meaningless, but they are certainly only secondary.

When we take a closer look at these distinctions, we can see that they are often motivated by the attempt to isolate one specific way to experience God and to position it against other ways in which God wants to interact with us.

YOUR THOUGHTS:

• *The three most important gift lists in the New Testament are Romans 12, 1 Corinthians 12, and Ephesians 4. Record the gifts that are mentioned in each list.*

Romans 12	1 Corinthians 12	Ephesians 4
Prophecy	Wisdom	Apostle
Serving others	Knowledge	Prophet
Teaching	Faith	Evangelist
Encouragement	Healing	Pastor
Giving	Miracles	Teacher
Leadership	Prophecy	
Kindness	Discernment	
	Tongues	
	Interpretation	

• *Which additional gifts can be found in the gift list on page 89?*

Hospitality   Counseling

Music   Singleness

Organization   Suffering

CHAPTER 2:
UNDERSTANDING
GIFTS

THREE DIFFERENT CATEGORIES OF GIFTS

In the past few years, I have discovered that most Christian groups have a system (whether developed consciously or not) for categorizing spiritual gifts. I have collected eight of these systems, ranging from those that distinguish between gifts that ceased to exist at the end of the apostolic age and gifts that are in effect today (basically, a two category system), to those that employ categories such as "motivational," "inspirational," and "functional" gifts (a three category system), to those with far more subtle distinctions that encompass many sub-categories.

IS CATEGORIZING SPIRITUAL GIFTS BIBLICAL?

It is interesting to note that most groups that teach one of these systems are convinced that the Bible proves their point of view. The truth is, however, that the Bible itself doesn't teach any of these categorizations. They are legitimate tools to systematize the many gifts that the New Testament mentions. Each of the systems that I have encountered stresses certain aspects and excludes others, depending on which aspects are important to the group in question.

THE DIFFERENT CATEGORIES REFLECT DIFFERENT ASPECTS OF GOD'S MINISTRY TO US. AT THE SAME TIME, THEY REFLECT DIFFERENT ASPECTS OF OUR MINISTRY TO OTHER PEOPLE.

If I divide spiritual gifts into three categories—those reflecting the green, red, and blue dimensions of the Christian faith—I have to stress that this system, like all the others, is not *the* biblical view, but simply another attempt to explain the multifaceted teaching of the New Testament. No one has to adopt this system. However, a trinitarian view of gifts can be quite helpful for discovering certain tendencies in our churches.

WHICH COLORS ARE PREDOMINANT IN YOUR CHURCH?

If you conduct the *Three-Color Gift Test*, you will discover in which of these three areas your personal gifting lies. For you as an individual this piece of information might not be that relevant since you can—and should!—simply accept the gifts that God has given to you, whether they are primarily green, red, or blue. You don't have to change your personal gift mix, because it reflects God's call for you. You might have primarily "red" gifts, while others have "blue" or "green" gifts—wonderful! However, if your whole church conducts the *Three-Color Gift Test,* it can be eye-opening to analyze as a whole body which colors are more represented than others. The results will probably reflect the culture of your church, including its blind spots.

We have already seen that different Christian traditions have an affinity for one, or maybe two, of the three colors (see diagram to the right). Frequently, though by no means always, this is also reflected in the gifts that predominate in individual churches within these traditions.

	Green segment	Red segment	Blue segment
Biblical paradigm	Creation	Calvary	Pentecost
Key term	work	word	wonder
Primary focus	world	Christ	church
Receptive group	liberals	evangelicals	charismatics

This table shows different tendencies regarding spiritual gifts that we find in various groups. Since God wants his church to reflect his fullness, he endows the church with gifts in all three areas.

WHY DO DIFFERENT CHURCHES HAVE DIFFERENT GIFT MIXES?

How can we explain the distribution of different spiritual gift mixes among churches? Is this by divine providence, or does it reflect our human one-sidedness (or even narrow-mindedness)? I believe that both can be true. It is quite natural for those gifts that are taught, expected, and encouraged in a given church to be discovered more readily than those gifts that are not part of the church's culture. If, for instance, social involvement is not an important issue in a given church, it is predictable that members won't discover as many gifts in the "green" area as they would in another context. If the dimension of the supernatural is regarded as unimportant, it is predictable that in such a church you won't find as many "blue" gifts as in others. And if winning people for Christ is not the priority of a church, we can predict that fewer gifts in the "red" area will be identified in that church than if the Great Commission were at the very center of the church's culture.

When using this trinitarian categorization, we must avoid thinking that different kinds of gifts are given by different "persons of the Godhead"—as if the Father bestows the green gifts; the Son, the red gifts; and the Holy Spirit, the blue gifts. No! All of the gifts are given by the same God, and all of them reflect different aspects of God's ministry to us. At the same time, they reflect different aspects of our ministry to other people.

YOUR THOUGHTS:

• *As you think about the gifts in each of the three categories, which colors are more strongly represented in your church?* RED

QUIZ: WHAT DO YOU KNOW ABOUT SPIRITUAL GIFTS?

In your opinion, are the statements below true or false? Mark the appropriate box.

True False

1. God rewards faithful Christians with spiritual gifts.

2. When a person receives a spiritual gift, it can be assumed that he or she will possess it their whole life.

3. Most, but not all, Christians have a spiritual gift.

4. Any Christian can receive any gift, if only he or she desires it.

5. There are always more Christians who don't have a specific gift than those who do have it.

6. God endows each Christian with the same gifts; only the manner in which they are utilized varies from person to person.

7. Every Christian should do his or her best to exercise all of the spiritual gifts mentioned in the New Testament.

8. In order not to become one-sided, Christians should be particularly active in those areas in which they do not possess any gifts.

9. Spiritual gifts are only present when there is no adequate natural explanation for an event.

10. The *Three-Color Gift Test* only needs to be taken once; the results apply for a lifetime.

11. The Bible clearly teaches that there are three categories of gifts that relate to the colors green, blue, and red.

12. A Christian should exercise his or her gifts but should not talk about them.

13. Anyone who holds a leadership position for which he or she does not have the corresponding gift should resign.

14. The only reason God gives us spiritual gifts is to deepen our personal relationship with him.

Answers:
1. F 2. T 3. F 4. F 5. T 6. F 7. F 8. F 9. F 10. F 11. F 12. F 13. T 14. F

HOW TO IDENTIFY YOUR SPIRITUAL GIFTS

The Bible teaches us that every Christian has at least one spiritual gift; nevertheless, 80 percent of all Christians cannot name their gifts. What can be done about this situation? The following steps can help everyone discover his or her spiritual gifts.

CHAPTER 3:
DISCOVERING
GIFTS

STEP 1: OPEN YOUR HEART TO GOD IN PRAYER

I n setting out to discover your spiritual gifts, it is important to bathe the entire process in prayer. Prayer is not an item to be accomplished and then checked off the list. Whether you are reading a book on spiritual gifts or are completing the *Three-Color Gift Test,* whether you are taking part in a workshop on spiritual gifts or are experimenting with a number of gifts, continually ask God, "What is it that you want to show me?"

ONLY TO THE DEGREE THAT YOU OPEN YOUR HEART TO GOD IN PRAYER WILL YOU BE ABLE TO MAKE NEW SPIR-ITUAL DISCOVERIES.

Many Christians have difficulty opening themselves up to God in prayer. They have a certain concept of spiritual gifts, and they are so focused on this concept that they cannot anticipate receiving new insights from God.

OPEN FOR NEW DISCOVERIES

When you are talking to God, open yourself up to him in such a way that he is able to do more than just confirm what you already know. Only through this kind of openness will you be able to make new spiritual discoveries.

YOUR THOUGHTS:

• *Are you open to all of the spiritual gifts mentioned in the Bible? Are there certain gifts that you would prefer not to have? If so, record those gifts here:*

• *Have you had any negative experiences with people exercising certain gifts? If so, bring those to God in prayer and ask him to release you so that those experiences do not hinder you in your own discovery process.*

• *Have you consciously asked God to use this manual to reveal to you your spiritual gifts? If not, why not do it now?*

STEP 2: BE READY TO APPLY YOUR GIFTS

Spiritual gifts are imparted to us so that we may accomplish certain tasks. Whoever is seriously interested in discovering his or her spiritual gifts must be open to applying them in building up the church.

Some time ago, a young man told me that he longed to receive the gift of healing. I asked him if he was prepared to use this gift in an ongoing prayer ministry for the sick. He shook his head, "No, I don't think I'm the right person for that kind of ministry."

"Why should God give you this gift if you're not prepared to put it to use?", I asked.

He responded, "I would just like to see what it feels like to have someone healed as a result of my prayers."

THE PROPER MOTIVATION

The desire to experience what it feels like to possess a certain gift is an understandable motive, but not a good one. Gifts are always given to serve others (1 Peter 4:10). If we are not willing to use certain gifts, why should God give them to us?

YOUR THOUGHTS:

• *Pick a gift from the gift list on page 89 which you suspect you might possess. If you cannot identify any gifts, then choose one that you would like to have. Record the gift below:*

• *How many hours per week are you prepared to invest toward the development and use of this gift?*

_____ *hours*

IF WE ARE NOT WILLING TO USE CERTAIN GIFTS, WHY SHOULD GOD GIVE THEM TO US?

STEP 3:
GET INFORMED

You will have difficulty determining which gifts are yours if you don't know what gifts exist. For this reason, it is important to learn about the gifts the Bible describes and about the exact meaning of the different terms. Collect as much information as possible.

Study what Scripture says about spiritual gifts. Discuss this in your small group. Talk to other Christians that you know possess a certain gift, and ask them how they discovered it. Read books about spiritual gifts. Study the explanation of the individual gifts in chapter 5 of this book.

LACK OF INFORMATION

YOU WILL HAVE DIFFICULTY DETERMINING WHICH GIFTS ARE YOURS IF YOU DON'T KNOW WHAT GIFTS EXIST.

A large percentage of the difficulties currently troubling many local churches stem from the fact that most Christians are simply uninformed regarding the divine principle of gift-based ministry. The good news is that this situation can be changed quite quickly. Thankfully, it is no longer very difficult to get relevant information on how to discover and utilize one's gifts.

YOUR THOUGHTS:

• *Write down the name of someone with whom you can discuss the gift you wrote down on page 61. (It is preferable to choose someone who has this gift.) How did he or she discover it? Take brief notes on their response.*

• *Read the information provided in chapter 5 regarding this gift. What characterizes people who have this gift?*

STEP 4: BEGIN WITH WHAT YOU ENJOY

There is an undying myth that a ministry is only a *real* ministry if the person ministering suffers in, through, and for it. A ministry that somebody enjoys is viewed suspiciously by many Christians.

Some time ago, when I did a seminar in a local church, an elderly lady approached me and said, "I've been involved in the children's ministry for 20 years, and I can tell you, I really don't like being around children. But I realize that it is not appropriate for me as a Christian to ask whether or not I enjoy something. The important thing is that God has called somebody to this ministry."

IT HAS ALWAYS BEEN GOD'S INTENTION THAT USING OUR SPIRITUAL GIFTS WOULD BRING US JOY.

Is it likely that God really did call this woman to this task? I rather doubt it. She suffers through each children's service, and according to what I heard from others in the church, the children's program she is responsible for is indeed a "catastrophe." As a result, this lady suffers, the children suffer, the parents suffer, the pastor suffers, and I am convinced that God suffers, too. This situation simply does not reflect his plan.

UTILIZING YOUR GIFTS BRINGS JOY

It is quite normal that putting your gifts into action brings you joy. Those with the gift of evangelism enjoy helping others come to faith. Those with the gift of hospitality enjoy taking guests into their homes. Those with the gift of service enjoy performing even those tasks that are not highly visible, as long as it builds up the church.

I have already mentioned that God has given me the gift of teaching. I really enjoy analyzing churches, developing graphic illustrations to communicate the results, preparing workshops, and then, best of all, spending hours and hours interacting with a group to find out how all of this can influence our lives. I can easily spend 12 to 16 hours a day on these kinds of activities, and I'm happy and satisfied with it. If I had to entertain guests for 12 hours a day—hospitality is not one of my gifts— it is likely that I'd suffer some sort of breakdown after two or three days. Yet there are those with the gift of hospitality who really thrive when they are placed in precisely such a situation.

JOY OR DUTY?

It has always been God's intention that using our spiritual gifts would bring us joy. Why? I believe it's because God knows that if we enjoy a certain task, we will naturally perform it much better. And the people with whom we are in regular contact will quickly notice if we are enthusiastic about a task or if we are just performing our "duty" in a tired and frustrated manner.

THE WHIM OF THE MOMENT

In short, if you want to discover your spiritual gifts, ask yourself, "What do I enjoy?" Don't confuse this, however, with the whim of the moment. Even though I have abundant joy in exercising my gifts, from time to time I will probably confront a situation in which I just want to throw in the towel. There have been many times when I have had absolutely no desire to carry through with an engagement, and I simply have had to force myself to do it.

This kind of experience doesn't contradict the statement that exercising your spiritual gifts brings joy. Everything that induces joy over the long haul requires hard work, and an occasional crisis is sure to come. I've learned from mountain climbers that they willingly endure great pain on their treks, and that they have to overcome many low points along the way. But it is precisely because of these extreme challenges that they experience a tremendous amount of satisfaction when they reach the summit—a feeling that people like me, who prefer riding the comfortable gondola, will never experience.

EVERYTHING THAT INDUCES JOY OVER THE LONG HAUL REQUIRES HARD WORK AND IS SURE TO INCLUDE AN OCCASIONAL CRISIS.

YOUR THOUGHTS:

* *Which tasks have brought you the most joy to date?*

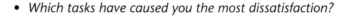

* *Which tasks have caused you the most dissatisfaction?*

* *Consider in greater detail the gift you chose on page 61. How do you feel when you are utilizing this gift?*

* *Which circumstances could make the utilization of this gift unpleasant?*

STEP 5: EXPERIMENT AS MUCH AS POSSIBLE

How are you going to discover whether or not you enjoy using a certain gift if you have never tried it? Maybe you already have the gift of giving, but since you have never exercised it, you have not yet discovered how much joy could be yours through sharing a significant portion of your income with others.

It is possible that you have the gift of evangelism but are not aware of it because you've never attempted to share the gospel with non-Christians.

It is just as possible that God has given you the gift of healing, but you don't know it because you have never prayed for the restoration of people's health.

If you aren't adventurous and willing to experiment, it is unlikely that you're going to track down your spiritual gift.

HOW ARE YOU GOING TO FIND OUT WHETHER YOU ENJOY USING A CERTAIN GIFT IF YOU HAVE NEVER TRIED IT?

YOUR THOUGHTS:

• *Consider once again the gift that you recorded on page 61. How can this gift be used? To which tasks have you already applied this gift? Which tasks would you like to try?*

• *Are you aware of any tasks that are not getting done? If so, which ones?*

• *Can you imagine being involved in these areas of ministry?*

• *Record here each of the gifts (listed on page 89) with which you have already experimented:*

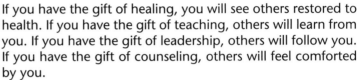

**CHAPTER 3:
DISCOVERING
GIFTS**

STEP 6: VERIFY YOUR EFFECTIVENESS

I f you suspect that you have the gift of evangelism, are active in this area, and yet year after year you are not leading anyone to faith in Christ, then there is good reason to doubt this supposition. If God has blessed you with the gift of evangelism, he will see to it that people come to faith through your efforts.

SPIRITUAL GIFTS ARE GIVEN TO PRO- DUCE CONCRETE RESULTS.

If you have the gift of healing, you will see others restored to health. If you have the gift of teaching, others will learn from you. If you have the gift of leadership, others will follow you. If you have the gift of counseling, others will feel comforted by you.

Spiritual gifts are given to produce results; thus, the evaluation of your effectiveness is a vital step in the gift discovery process.

YOUR THOUGHTS:

- *Record here the effect that the exercise of each gift should yield.*

Gift	Effect
Healing	*People are restored to health*
Prophecy	
Organization	
Hospitality	
Prayer	
Music	

- *What results have occurred as you have applied the gift you wrote down on page 61?*

STEP 7: SEEK THE OPINION OF OTHERS

I know Christians who are 100 percent convinced that God has blessed them with a certain gift. They have prayed intensely about it (indeed, this kind of prayer is one of their favorite activities); they are ready to apply the gift (whether it is appropriate or not); they know all about the hidden secrets behind this gift (usually far more than you can find in the Bible); they enjoy their task (they simply are not able to hide this); they have experimented a lot (being really risky and not caring whether or not some of their experiments have done harm); and they perceive their ministry as being extremely effective. The problem is that they are the only ones that see it that way. Such a situation should cause one to become skeptical.

Other people, from your own church and beyond, should provide confirmation of your gifts.

YOUR THOUGHTS:

• *What should be the characteristics of people who can help others confirm their gifts?*

• *Write down the name of a person who could help you confirm the gift you named on page 61.*

• *When will you talk with him or her about it?*

OTHER PEOPLE, FROM YOUR OWN CHURCH AND BEYOND, SHOULD PROVIDE CONFIRMATION OF YOUR GIFTS.

THE THREE-COLOR GIFT TEST

eTest

Gift Profile

ONLINE

3colorsofyourgifts.org

Before you take the *Three-Color Gift Test* now, it is important for you to understand that the test is not meant to substitute, but to complement the seven discovery steps described on pages 60–67. I am well aware that, in spite of this warning, many readers will abstain from dealing with the seven steps. Following that path, the whole gift discovery process will be reduced to about an hour of sitting in front of the computer, answering questions and reading the evaluation.

I cannot stop anyone from taking that approach. However, by doing so, it is predetermined that you will not see the results the test was designed for—finding out one's spiritual calling. But this is exactly what I want to encourage you to explore. Therefore, the test should be embedded into a comprehensive discovery process, including prayer and study, experiments and conversations. The value of the actual test will increase to the degree that you seriously invest in the discovery process described.

A RELIABLE RESULT

TRY TO BE HONEST WITH YOURSELF—ONLY THEN WILL THE RESULTS PROVIDE YOU WITH AN ACCURATE BASIS FOR DEVELOPING YOUR GIFTS IN THE DAYS AHEAD.

Throughout the past years, we have invested a lot of energy in developing an internationally applicable test procedure yielding results that are as precise as possible. When you take the online test, you won't notice this background work. You will simply answer 180 questions and ask some people to fill in a short online questionnaire for you. Then you press *Finalize and calculate eTest,* and you will receive an extensive evaluation. The mathematical formulae calculating the results are based on a quite complex normation process, which is constantly refined, reflecting the increasing amount of data available to us.

Because of that procedure, you can rely on the fact that the results will be "correct"—i.e. they are as exact as possible within an incomplete world. However, you have to consider that the test can only evaluate experiences that you have gained in the past. If you have never been involved in certain tasks, even the best test in the world cannot tell you if you may have gifts in the respective area (even if we have worked on addressing this situation, at least to a certain degree, with the introduction of "latent gifts," described on page 70). That is the chief background for us to encourage ongoing experimentation in our "seven step program."

DISCOVERING ONE'S UNIQUE CALLING

I have repeatedly been asked why we invest so much energy in the preciseness of the test. The question is easy to answer. Many people plan their lives on the basis of the test results—their job, their continuing education, their church involvement, their commitment to more justice in the world. A wrong or imprecise result could have disastrous consequences. For us, the preciseness of the test results is a profoundly ethical question.

HOW TO CONDUCT THE ETEST

The fact that the *Three-Color Gift Test* is available as an eTest, enables you to get your results quicker and easier than ever before. Simply stick to the following four steps:

STEP 1: GO ONLINE

Visit *www.ncd-tools.org/mycode* and insert the access code that is printed on the bookmark attached to this book. You will be automatically guided through the process. You will need to either log in to your existing 3 Color World account or create a new one. Once you have completed those steps, you will arrive on the eTests page. Then, click the button to take the Gift Test. Conducting one *Three-Color Gift Test* is already included in the price of the book; in addition to it your bookmark code gives you access to one additional test, which is a gift from us. If you would like to do more tests in the future, you can purchase additional tokens at any given time.

STEP 2: REQUEST FEEDBACK FROM OTHERS

You will be asked to type in the names and e-mail addresses of some people that should know you well. As a minimum, this must be two people, but you are free to invite as many people as you want. We recommend you invite 5–10 people. Each person will then receive an email invitation to fill in an online questionnaire consisting of 30 questions (taking about 6 minutes). You may wish to use the invitation text suggested, you may alter it, or write a completely new one. Whenever one of these people completes the survey, you will be automatically informed. At no point throughout the process will you see the individual answers that these people have given.

STEP 3: COMPLETE YOUR RESPONSES

You will be forwarded to a page with 180 questions. Please answer as spontaneously as possible and try to be honest.

STEP 4: CALCULATE RESULTS

Once at least two people you invited in Step 2 have answered the questions, you can click on *Finalize and calculate eTest*. You will then receive a detailed evaluation of your personal gift profile (see page 70–72).

A GROUP PROFILE WILL PROVIDE YOU WITH HIGHLY RELEVANT INSIGHTS INTO THE POTENTIAL OF THE WHOLE CHURCH, WHICH ARE OF IMMENSE VALUE FOR ANY PLANNING PROCESS.

CONSIDER A GROUP PROFILE

If you are part of a Christian group or a church, you should consider a group profile. Every participant fills in the *Three-Color Gift Test* and receives his or her personal result. In addition, there will be an evaluation for the group as a whole. A group profile will provide you highly relevant insights in the potential of your group or church, which are of immense value for any planning process.

CHAPTER 3:
DISCOVERING
GIFTS

UNDERSTANDING THE RESULTS

The gift profile you will receive as a result of the *Three-Color Gift Test* will provide you with a lot of insights. It is helpful to distinguish four levels of interpretation:

LEVEL 1: THREE SPIRITUAL GIFTS

As long as the Gift Test was only available in printed form, every participant inserted into a box the gifts with the highest scores. These were very likely the "spiritual gifts" that they should focus on. Essentially, this was the information that older versions of the Gift Test provided.

Even if the gift profile based on the eTest enables much deeper—and also, more complex—evaluations, some users would like to simply identify the three (or five or seven) gifts with the highest scores. In the new evaluation manual, you will find this basic information, just as before, right in the beginning of the profile. If you are not interested in the more advanced information that the profile provides, simply disregard that part of the profile.

LEVEL 2: MANIFEST AND LATENT GIFTS

THE THREE-COLOR EVALUATION CAN ALERT YOU TO POTENTIAL ONE-SIDEDNESSES.

On page 68 it has already been mentioned that the test—which primarily evaluates experiences gained in the past—can only identify gifts in areas in which you have been active before. We call them *manifest gifts*. These are gifts that you have already seen in action in your life and which have been confirmed by others. When it comes to adopting a specific task—be it at church or beyond—you should focus on these gifts.

In addition, the gift profile will draw your attention to what we call *latent gifts*. These are gifts that haven't become manifest in your life yet, but which you may identify as spiritual gifts at the moment you become active in the respective ministry area. You should deliberately look for possibilities to "experiment" with these gifts (see page 65).

This diagram indicates how strongly developed each of the spiritual gifts are in your life (or in the life of a whole group). Your spiritual gifts are toward the left-hand end of the chart.

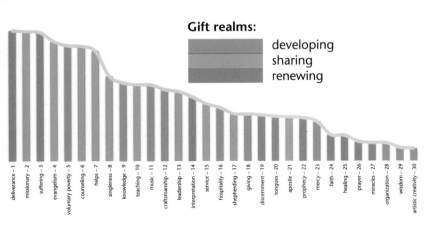

Gift realms:

developing
sharing
renewing

deliverance – 1
missionary – 2
suffering – 3
evangelism – 4
voluntary poverty – 5
counselling – 6
helps – 7
singleness – 8
knowledge – 9
teaching – 10
music – 11
craftsmanship – 12
leadership – 13
interpretation – 14
service – 15
hospitality – 16
shepherding – 17
giving – 18
discernment – 19
tongues – 20
apostle – 21
prophecy – 22
mercy – 23
faith – 24
healing – 25
prayer – 26
miracles – 27
organization – 28
wisdom – 29
artistic creativity – 30

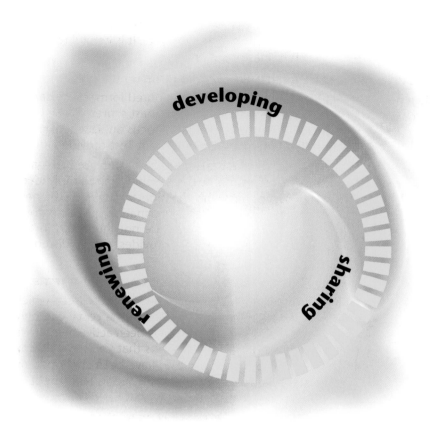

developing

sharing

renewing

This book distinguishes three different categories of gifts, which correspond to the colors green, red, and blue: developing, sharing, and renewing gifts. It is highly relevant, both for individuals and for whole groups/churches, to analyze which of these three categories is strongest, and which one is the weakest.

LEVEL 3: THREE-COLOR EVALUATION

As explained on pages 56–57, the *Three-Color Gift Test* distinguishes three categories of gifts: developing gifts (green), sharing gifts (red), and renewing gifts (blue). Take a look at the graphic above. It indicates that this person has a stronger tendency to the sharing gifts, while the developing and the renewing gifts are less developed. This kind of evaluation can alert you to potential one-sidednesses. Every group tends to certain "favorite colors," which are considered more important than the others.

Please notice that, when a three-color evaluation is produced, not only the gifts with the highest scores are included (whether these are three or five or seven), but the answers to *all* questions answered while completing the *Three-Color Gift Test.* Even if you have answered some of the questions with "not at all" or "hardly" (which is an indication that these are not spiritual gifts), all of these answers are included in a three-color evaluation.

LEVEL 4: GROUP PROFILE

Once all group participants have done the eTest, you can create, in addition to the individual results, a group profile. If you are interested in this option, you should consider planning the gift discovery exercise as a group process from the outset, as this makes the technical procedure considerably easier for you. You will find further information at *www.3colorworld.org/etests*. Particularly at the level of a group profile, a three-color evaluation can be extremely eye-opening.

> **EVERY PERSON AND EVERY GROUP TENDS TO HAVE A CERTAIN FAVORITE COLOR, WHICH IS CONSIDERED MORE IMPORTANT THAN THE OTHERS.**

At NCD International, we have the highest imaginable standards in terms of the privacy of data. Nobody will ever see your results with the exception of you—and those people with whom you would like to share them. Conversely, you will at no time see the individual answers of the people who have filled in an external questionnaire for you.

Diagram below: The gift profile doesn't only reveal the "favorite color" of an individual or group, but indicates at the same time which sub-category in each of the color areas is most developed. On pages 92–124 you will find more information on every single gift mentioned in the table.

DEVELOPING			SHARING			RENEWING		

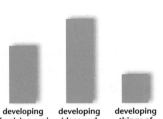
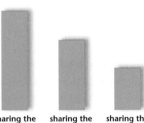
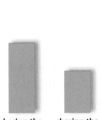

developing life-giving environments:	developing ideas and systems:	developing things of purpose and beauty:	sharing the good news:	sharing the way forward:	sharing the load:	renewing trust in God:	renewing connections with God:	renewing through the power of God:
giving	knowledge	artistic creativity	evangelism	apostle	helps	faith	discernment	deliverance
hospitality	organization	craftsmanship	missionary	counseling	service	prayer	interpretation	healing
mercy	wisdom	music		leadership	singleness	suffering	prophecy	miracles
voluntary poverty				shepherding			tongues	
				teaching				

PRACTICAL STEPS

As important as it is to get an increasingly deeper understanding of one's own gift profile, as long as you don't draw practical consequences out of these insights, the whole process won't be much more than a purely academic exercise. My experience is that especially Protestants—who have, for good reasons, a high view of the "word"—are in danger of confusing talking about certain topics with the process of practical implementation.

TALKING DOESN'T MEAN IMPLEMENTING

Just listen in to the following conversation that I had a while ago with a protestant pastor.

Pastor: We have done NCD in our church, but it didn't work.

Christian: What have you done?

Pastor: Well, the Church Profile. And our minimum factor was gift-based ministry.

Christian: I see. And what exactly have you done to strategically improve the quality in that area?

Pastor: We have appointed a committee that dealt with the topic for eight months. But it didn't work.

Christian: That was not my question. My question was, what have you actually done.

In many cases, the answer to the question would be "nothing"—even if the committee did "work" intensively. It may have analyzed the profile and interpreted it from all different angles (which is an extremely valuable foundation from which to select the most relevant practical steps), but it has completely failed to put anything into practice. And even if some measures are taken, many churches fail to stick to the process consistently. The most frequent mistake in the area of gift-based ministry is to reduce one's activities to mere gift discovery, rather than proactively and consistently nurturing the process of helping people invest their spiritual gifts in fitting tasks.

WHILE MANY COMMITTEES ARE GOOD AT EXPLORING THE QUESTIONS AT STAKE, THEY FAIL TO DRAW THE NECESSARY PRACTICAL CONSEQUENCES.

STEP 1:
GIFT ACTIVATION—YOUR RESPONSIBILITY

If you have identified your spiritual gifts with the help of the *Three-Color Gift Test,* it is your responsibility to put your gifts into practice. Don't wait until other people—for instance, your pastor—approach you. Become proactive. And if nobody shows an interest in you ministering in the area of your giftedness, look for opportunities beyond your local church to use your gifts for the benefit of others. People who have discovered their gifts without using them, will become more dissatisfied in the long run than those who have never discovered their gifts.

On the other hand, if you have leadership responsibility in your church, it is of course your responsibility to help church members find a task that matches their spiritual gifts. In this process it is a helpful rule of thumb not to start with the "tasks that have to be done," but with the identified gifts of your people, and *then* ask: "What kind of tasks would be most adequate for living out these gifts?"

On *www.3colorsofyourgifts.org* you will find resources that can assist you in this process (for instance, a handbook for gift counselors).

STEP 2:
A COMMUNAL ENTERPRISE

In the Western world in particular, people tend to misunderstand Christianity as a business of individualists. Throughout the first parts of this book it should have become clear that we can neither discover our gifts nor use them in a meaningful way, as long as we withdraw ourselves from community.

One of the easiest ways of approaching gift-activation as a communal enterprise is a several-week gift discovery process for your whole group. Or you start a new group exclusively with those interested in discovering their spiritual gifts. And please don't reduce the activities to mere gift discovery. As long as each participant has not found a task that matches his or her gift mix, the process has to continue. On *www.3colorsofyourgifts.org* you will find resources that can support you in this process (for instance a handbook for small group leaders that enables them to lead their participants through a process of gift-activation).

ONLY IN COMMU-NITY WITH OTHERS CAN WE EXPECT TO LIVE OUT OUR SPIRITUAL GIFTS.

STEP 3:
SHARING WHAT YOU HAVE RECEIVED

It is a basic law of spirituality to share what we have received with others. If you have discovered your spiritual gifts and have become happier and more effective in this process, you should help others to experience the same thing. This applies in particular to those who have high energy in the area of "identity" (see page 18). People with high identity energy should see one of their major responsibilities as supporting gift-activation within their respective environment.

This is the major reason why the access code, that is printed on the bookmark, enables you to do not only one eTest, but two. The first one has been acquired as part of purchasing the book. The second test, however, is a gift from us. Of course, you are free to use the second token for yourself (for instance, in order to take a repeat-profile after a certain time in order check if something has changed). But, via the web site, you can also use the second token to invite someone else to take the Gift Test.

A picture that I use in almost all of my seminars: All of these people are moving in the same direction, which is, toward the center. But depending on their respective starting points they have to take different, sometimes even opposite, paths in order to reach this destination.

AN EXERCISE THAT BRINGS THE BIBLE TO LIFE

Have a look at the graphic above. If you are already familiar with Natural Church Development, you may have encountered this picture in other contexts before. It expresses in a graphical way what the Trinitarian Compass is all about. All people that you see in this picture are moving in the same direction, which is, toward the center. When translating these dynamics from the symbolic language of this image into reality, it means that everyone is moving toward God, who is at the center of the Trinitarian Compass. However, depending on their respective starting points they have to take different paths—sometimes even opposite paths—to reach that destination.

Whenever the situation allows for it, I try to demonstrate these dynamics in seminars and conferences. It is one thing to meditate on such a graphic and to deepen one's insights through intellectual reflection. But it is something altogether different to *experience* yourself—together with a whole group or church—as part of the Trinitarian Compass. Therefore I would like to encourage you to do the following exercise (which you may adapt according to your needs) together with your whole group or church:

- All participants have both the results of the *Change Compass* (pages 38–41) and the results of the *Three-Color Gift Test* (pages 68–69) at hand.

- You start by giving a short introduction to the six starting points (Thomas, Martha, Mary, Moses, Peter, Jonah) and the topic of spiritual gifts (one body—many parts). You can summarize the main topics by projecting the pictures of pages 41 and 75, on the wall. On *www.3colorsofyourgifts.org* you will find these and other pictures for free download.

- You produce six posters with the names Thomas, Martha, Mary, Moses, Peter and Jonah and attach them, arranged in a circle corresponding to their position within the Trinitarian Compass, to the wall. You ask the participants to walk to the poster with the name of their biblical "model."

- As a group leader you can move to the center of the circle and explain the following four dynamics: (1) Your group encompasses many diverse starting points, with some more strongly represented than others. (2) Every single person in the room is, just like the six biblical models, one-sided; no human being, with the exception of Jesus, is completely in balance. (3) There are neighboring positions (e.g. Thomas/Jonah) and opposite positions (e.g. Thomas/Peter). (4) It is the task of every person to move closer to the center. In practical terms this means to learn from the opposite position. Take sufficient time to illustrate each of the four points by examples taken from the group gathered in the room, for instance by interviews with individual group members.

THOMAS, MARTHA, MARY, MOSES, PETER, AND JONAH ARE RIGHT IN OUR MIDST.

- Now every participant approaches a person that is positioned approximately opposite to him or herself (e.g. Thomas/Peter, Mary/Martha).

- The representatives of the the opposite poles share, in dialogue between two people each, about their experiences with God. They strive to find out how they can support each other in spiritual growth.

- After this warming-up exercise the participants share, in the same pairs, about their respective gift profiles: Related to spiritual gifts, is there a color that is stronger represented? Could this be my personal favorite color? What is the relationship between the colors of the Change Compass to those of the gift profile? (Some people have, in both cases, a similar color mix, for others, the colors in both cases differ; both are meaningful discoveries. While the gift profile provides an answer to the question, *What should be done?*, the *Character Compass* addresses the question, *How will I do it?*) What can we practically do to use our respective gifts better than before?

You will find resources for working with groups (such as, the pictures and diagrams of this book) at: 3colorsofyourgifts. org

Whenever I have done this exercise with a group of people, it was as if Thomas, Martha, Mary, Moses, Peter and Jonah were right in our midst. This is one of those exercises that help bring the Bible to life. Scripture is not (only) about things that happened more than 2,000 years ago, but (also) about things that happen here and now.

LEARNING TO UTILIZE YOUR GIFTS

Something decisive has happened—you have discovered your spiritual gifts. At least you are now aware of the areas in which God has most likely gifted you. It is important to remember, however, that the discovery of one's gifts is not an end in itself. Rather, it reveals the tasks to which God has called you, and therefore expects your involvement. But how can spiritual gifts be applied in such a way that they help your church grow?

THE THREE-COLOR CHURCH

It is not God's plan that individual believers reflect his fullness all by themselves. Each of us is only a *part* of the body of Christ, and we *have* to be different in order to complement each other. But it *is* God's plan that the body as a whole—his church—reflects his fullness. If a color is excluded from a church's life, it may be an indication that something is out of balance. If your personal gifts are exclusively in the red area, this does not mean that your life is out of balance. It may reflect precisely God's will for you. However, if your whole church excludes a certain color, it is a different story. By identifying the kinds of gifts that are predominant in your church, you will discover its areas for future growth.

BY IDENTIFYING THE KINDS OF GIFTS THAT ARE PREDOMINANT IN YOUR CHURCH, YOU WILL DISCOVER ITS AREAS FOR FUTURE GROWTH.

THE "COLOR BLEND" OF YOUR CHURCH

Do you already know in which of the three colors your church is strong and in which areas it might be underdeveloped? It may be that different members of your church have different opinions about this topic. However, we should not confuse opinions with reality. What color(s) does your church *really* reflect? The best way to gather reliable information on this topic is to collect the results of the *Three-Color Gift Test* for the whole church. Through the website *3colorsofyourgifts.org* this is quite easy. Once you have the results you can see at first glance, which color is predominant and which colors present opportunities for future growth. I have done this kind of exercise quite often in different churches, and I have discovered that the results often surprise people.

Of course, the number of gifts that appear in each of the three areas is only one of many indicators of your church's color blend. Another indication might be found in a corporate analysis of the *Change Compass* (pages 38–41), and still other indicators in a study of your church's core values, its devotional style, and so forth.

Analyzing the distribution of spiritual gifts with regard to the three colors is one of the most objective tools for determining your church's starting point. As I have tried to show on pages 56 and 57 of this book, it is quite natural that if the teaching in your church focuses on certain areas more than on others, the members will be more likely to discover gifts in those areas. If this assumption is true, then analyzing the distribution of gifts within your church can help you discover the actual impact of your church's teaching.

YOUR THOUGHTS:

• *If your church has done the Three-Color Gift Test, what color(s) is/are most represented? Is this result what you expected?*

FUTURE GROWTH AREAS FOR YOUR CHURCH

O nce we know where we are, we can determine where we want to go. Let's assume that your church is particularly strong in one (or two) of the three colors. Future growth doesn't mean that you have to leave your area(s) of strength. Rather, you should add new dimensions to your life and teaching so that your church more fully reflects the triune God.

Many believers are afraid of this kind of growth because they are not accustomed to it. The unknown can cause one of two emotions in us: fear or curiosity. Since we are speaking here of nothing less than reflecting God's nature, my hope and prayer is that the feeling of curiosity will override that of fear.

NEGATIVE EXPERIENCES WITH OTHER GROUPS

However, there is one thing that can be a real hindrance to this growth process. Every Christian has had exposure to other Christian groups, and not all of these experiences have been positive. In my seminars I have discovered that as long as I restrict myself to teaching about the triune God, his threefold revelation, and how we can reflect the three colors in our lives, almost everybody agrees. But as soon as I make explicit references to different Christian groups, such as evangelicals, charismatics, or liberals, I sense feelings of anxiety and rejection among the participants. I then hear statements like these:

- "If reflecting the color blue means becoming like this or that charismatic church, we definitely aren't interested."

- "We have had enough experiences with evangelical churches that stress the color red to know that this is not the right thing for us."

- "You can only speak that naively about the green segment because you have never encountered the disastrous consequences of liberal theology."

Can you see what is happening here? Rather than looking at the triune God and asking, "How can we better reflect his fullness in our church?" we look at different churches, identify their limitations, and then, understandably, come to the conclusion that this is not the right thing for us. Starting the process with these kinds of negative perceptions blocks us from experiencing God in a new way. This is one of the great tragedies of Christianity.

ONCE WE KNOW WHERE WE ARE, WE CAN DETERMINE WHERE WE WANT TO GO.

CONCENTRATE ON THE NATURE OF GOD, NOT ON HIS PEOPLE!

If you associate primarily negative feelings with the terms "charismatic," "evangelical," or "liberal," my counsel is that you forget these names. You don't have to become "charismatic" (in the same way as some wild, arrogant churches that you know) in order to reflect the color blue. You don't have to become "evangelical" (in the same way as some narrow-minded, legalistic churches) in order to reflect the color red. And you don't have to become "liberal" (in the same way as some fully syncretistic churches that don't appear Christian at all) in order to reflect the color green. The point is not to imitate other Christian groups, but rather to learn from the different aspects of God's nature and to consider what they might mean for the life of your church.

YOU CANNOT PRO-DUCE SPIRITUAL GIFTS, BUT YOU CAN CREATE A CLIMATE IN WHICH CERTAIN GIFTS CAN GROW.

My counsel is simply this: When thinking about future growth areas for your church, don't begin by reflecting on other Christian groups. Rather, begin by meditating on the nature of the triune God! If you follow this advice, I trust you may discover that the three colors communicate something completely different to you.

THE SPIRITUAL CLIMATE

Let's assume that your church agrees with what we've said so far. Let's also assume that you have already identified which color is most strongly represented in your church. Furthermore, let's assume that you have decided that you would like to grow in the other areas. Now what do you do? If gifts from a certain category are missing in your church, or are underdeveloped, you cannot simply "add" them, because you are not God. No one can produce spiritual gifts, but what you can do is create a climate in which certain gifts can grow.

YOUR THOUGHTS:

• *List several ways in which your church could grow in the color segments that seem to be underdeveloped right now.*

THE MINISTRY DESCRIPTION

Whenever you discover a specific gift—it might be in the green, red, or blue area—it is important that you use it; in other words, that you apply it to prevailing needs. Find out where your gifts are most urgently needed.

I am always surprised at how little most churches take to heart the simple idea that gifts and tasks must correspond to one another. For example, I'm not aware of many instances in which the spiritual gifts of church leaders are consistently taken into account. Instead, completely different criteria are considered more important. For this reason, it is little wonder that the *wrong* people so frequently fill these positions, that is, people that God hasn't gifted for these offices.

GIFTS AND TASKS MUST CORRESPOND

To ensure that gifts and tasks in a church complement one another, it is necessary that a description be drafted for each area of ministry. Just what does this mean? Actually, it's very simple. The responsibilities relating to each task should be written down. A collection of these ministry descriptions will help interested individuals determine at first glance what might be expected of them, how time-consuming the task might be, which gifts and abilities are being sought, and what training is necessary.

FIND OUT WHERE YOUR GIFTS ARE MOST URGENTLY NEEDED.

CLARIFYING THE MINISTRY DESCRIPTION

The following points should be clearly defined in each ministry description:

- *What is involved:* Every task is made up of sub-tasks. It is important to clarify all the details necessary for each of these sub-tasks. Therefore, make sure that the tasks for which you are responsible are clearly defined, and that they are not expanded without changing the ministry description.

- *Necessary training*: What kind of training is necessary or required to effectively carry out this task? Who will organize the training? When?

- *Spiritual gifts desired:* Which spiritual gifts are preferred to carry out this task? Answer this question for each sub-task.

- *Desired talents:* Which additional abilities are most important for the task at hand? Which interests? Experiences? These questions should also be answered for each of the corresponding sub-tasks.

- *Contact people:* Should questions or problems arise, to whom can workers turn? When? How?

- *Length of assignment:* Failing to provide a definite termination point is a common error. It is important to limit the time period for each task and to discuss at the end of this period the option of extending the length of involvement. In short, make sure that any ministry tasks you assume are time-bound.

YOUR THOUGHTS:

• *What are the tasks that would best utilize the gifts that you have discovered (both your manifest and latent gifts)?*

Manifest gifts   **Possible tasks**

Latent gifts   **Possible tasks**

• *Develop a ministry description for each of the tasks you are presently involved in or wish to be involved in, in the future. The following form demonstrates how easy this is. You'll find a blank form on page 144. Don't forget to discuss this ministry description with the appropriate contact person.*

EXAMPLE OF A MINISTRY DESCRIPTION

Task	Date
Leading an open small group	January 27, 2017

Goals
Reach out to unchurched people; Help them get to know Christ; Integrate them into the church; Multiply leadership team within 9 months; Start a new group

Sub-tasks
Develop a group strategy based on the "The 3 Colors of Community" (together with the small-group coordinator); Establish a leadership team and provide training; Select a co-leader

Contact people	
Responsible for:	Small group members and leadership team
Responsible to:	Small group coordinator and pastor
Work with:	Leader of evangelism

Spiritual gifts	Abilities/Interests
Shepherding and/or leadership	Positive attitude
possibly evangelism	Relationship-oriented
possibly teaching	Openness, transparency

Time commitment	Length of assignment
approx. 8 hours/week	4 months (February to May)

Training
Participate in 14-day training "The 3 Colors of Leadership"; Participate in course "The 3 Colors of Community" 1 and 2; Visit two experienced NCD churches

Additional agreements

USE AND ABUSE

According to the New Testament, each gift is to be used to build up the body of Christ (cf. 1 Cor. 14:12). Unfortunately, this criterion is not always given adequate consideration, which has resulted in countless examples of the misuse of spiritual gifts.

WITHOUT EXCEPTION, EACH GIFT CAN BE MISUSED IF IT IS NOT APPLIED TO CHURCH DEVELOPMENT.

Each gift, without exception, can be misused if it is not applied to church development. This is not an indictment against the respective gift, but rather an indictment against the improper application of it.

At the same time, the reverse is equally true, i.e., that each gift—without exception—can be used for church development.

HOW TO AVOID MISUSE

Misuse of spiritual gifts can not be prevented by "forbidding" certain gifts. Misuse can only be prevented by demonstrating creative ways to properly use each gift so that it benefits others, builds up the body of Christ, and brings glory to God.

YOUR THOUGHTS:

• *Not every church activity contributes to the building up of the body of Christ. However, you should concentrate on tasks which serve to this end. Brainstorm how the gifts you have identified as your own can contribute to church development.*

Gift	Usefulness for church development
_____	_____
_____	_____
_____	_____
_____	_____
_____	_____

TRAIN YOUR GIFTS

E ven though God has given you certain gifts, this doesn't imply that there isn't room for improvement in these areas. On the contrary, you should make every effort to train these gifts so that they can be used to their fullest potential (cf. 2 Tim. 1:6). Participate in seminars that will equip you. Gain further experience. Learn from the constructive criticism of others. Allow God to constantly shape and change you.

AN ONGOING GROWTH PROCESS

Since I've discovered that I have the gift of teaching, I've invested a considerable amount of time in training. I am particularly conscious of how much I still have to learn in this area. I like to hear Christians who have this gift to a greater degree than I. I regularly attend training sessions on communication skills, which help me to improve the use of my gift. I appreciate it when others offer a realistic critique of my efforts. I ask God to keep showing me new insights which will better equip me to help others understand important spiritual dynamics. And I am counting on the fact that in ten years I will be able to exercise my gift much better than I do today.

YOU SHOULD MAKE EVERY EFFORT TO TRAIN YOUR GIFTS TO THEIR FULLEST POTENTIAL.

YOUR THOUGHTS:

• *Name some ways in which you can train to improve the effectiveness of your gifts. If you have difficulty coming up with possibilities on your own, discuss this question with someone in your church who is responsible for the ministry areas in which you are gifted. Read the suggestions in chapter 5 which are provided for each gift. Record precisely what you plan to do in this area over the next few months.*

Gift	Possibilities for training
_____	_____
_____	_____
_____	_____
_____	_____
_____	_____

CHAPTER 4:
APPLYING
GIFTS

REMAIN OPEN TO ADDITIONAL GIFTS

I t would be misleading to view the discovery of your gifts as a process that ends at a certain point in time and that remains valid for all eternity.

Some theologians hold the view that a Christian receives all of his or her gifts at conversion—subsequently the issue becomes merely the *discovery* of these gifts. Others emphasize that God can give us new gifts which we didn't previously possess. According to this line of thought, it is not a matter of discovering gifts, but rather of *receiving* them.

PERHAPS SOME-DAY GOD WILL GIVE YOU GIFTS ABOUT WHICH YOU KNOW NOTHING TODAY.

Personally, I find this dispute of little value. Regardless of whether our gifts are newly discovered or newly endowed, the important point is that we don't view our gift mix as static, but that we remain open to new discoveries.

SEEKING NEW GIFTS

Paul admonishes Christians to "eagerly desire" gifts (1 Cor. 12:31 and 14:1). When a church recognizes that the gifts presently being exercised in a given task are not adequate, it needs to pray that God will bless those involved in ministry with new gifts or send new workers who possess the gifts that are lacking.

YOUR THOUGHTS:

• *You have identified certain latent gifts in the Three-Color Gift Test. There is reason to believe that God may show you new manifest gifts in these areas. Therefore, pay particular attention to them and experiment with them in the near future.*

• *Gifts are not static. For this reason, it is wise to repeat the Three-Color Gift Test from time to time, especially when you go through phases in which God is uniquely working in your life. Record below when you plan to take the Three-Color Gift Test a second time.*

THE DANGER OF GIFT PROJECTION

Every Christian tends to project his or her gifts onto others. I tend to do this, and you probably will have the same tendency. For example, those with the gift of hospitality very often cannot understand why others, like me, have so much difficulty in this area. They may say, "It's so easy." Undoubtedly, they are right. Practicing hospitality is easy—for them. They simply cannot imagine how draining a task it is for those who don't have this gift.

WATCH OUT!

The phenomenon of gift projection is particularly prevalent in the area of evangelism. Many Christians with this gift deny that it is a special gift from God. They maintain, "God has not given me a special gift. I'm only doing what every Christian should do." In saying this, they cause those without this gift to have a guilty conscience. The truth is, not every Christian can reach out evangelistically the way they do. They can do it because they have the corresponding gift. Others cannot do it since God has given them different gifts.

EVERYONE TENDS TO PROJECT HIS OR HER GIFTS ONTO OTHERS.

YOUR THOUGHTS:

• *Just like every other Christian, you will tend to project your gifts onto others. For each of the gifts you have discovered, write down a few examples of when and where you may have expected others to act in a way that can only be expected of those who have the corresponding gift.*

_____   _____

_____   _____

_____   _____

_____   _____

_____   _____

CHAPTER 4:
APPLYING
GIFTS

GIFTS AND THE WHIM OF THE MOMENT

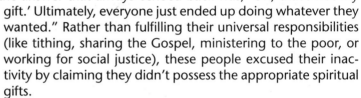

After I had lectured on spiritual gifts at a seminar, a pastor approached me and said, "You can forget all that gift ideology of yours. I tried it in my church for a period of time, and it resulted in catastrophe. If the discussion focused on some less desirable ministry, the answer that always echoed back was, 'Oh, that's not my gift.' Ultimately, everyone just ended up doing whatever they wanted." Rather than fulfilling their universal responsibilities (like tithing, sharing the Gospel, ministering to the poor, or working for social justice), these people excused their inactivity by claiming they didn't possess the appropriate spiritual gifts.

GIFT-BASED MINISTRY DOESN'T MEAN "JUST DOING WHAT I WANT."

Gift-based ministry doesn't mean "just doing what I want." Rather, it means allowing God to determine when and where he wants to use us. How is it possible that this teaching could be so misunderstood?

THE DANGER OF SELF-JUSTIFICATION

My suspicion is that all of us tend to make our lives as comfortable as possible. Thus, any theory that could somehow justify this interest is welcomed. It's entirely possible that teaching on spiritual gifts will be used to this end, too. Yes, it must be twisted quite a bit to make it fit for this purpose, but who cares?

Whenever the gift-based approach is confused with the whim of the moment, self-justification is right around the corner.

YOUR THOUGHTS:

• *Look at the list of gifts once again, paying particular attention to the gifts you don't have (see page 89). Remember, for each of these gifts there are corresponding "universal responsibilities" (as described on page 52). You cannot ignore these basic roles. Write down which of these responsibilities gives you the greatest difficulty.*

• *What can you do to avoid the danger of self-justification?*

BACKGROUNDS, DEFINITIONS, PRACTICAL TIPS

Please identify which of the gifts listed below are your

✘ *"manifest" or*

♪ *"latent" gifts.*

Then study the explanations that correspond to your personal gift mix.

HOW TO STUDY
THE INDIVIDUAL GIFTS

This chapter will help you study the individual gifts in greater detail. Rather than reading the whole chapter page after page, you may want to begin with your manifest and latent gifts. Each page of explanation uses the following pattern:

CATEGORY

Each of the gifts is related to one of the three categories described in this book. This is not because that gift is *exclusively* related to that area, but because one color seems to predominate while the others are in the background. Furthermore, while a gift may correspond primarily to a certain color, it should still be exercised in a three-colored way. These considerations are important to keep in mind when dealing with your personal gift mix. For example, let's suppose that one of your gifts is artistic creativity (green category). How can you exercise a predominantly green gift in a three-colored way? Aside from perfecting your artistic skill (growth in wisdom), you should intentionally seek ways to use this gift for kingdom purposes (growth in commitment) and ask God to maximize your efforts for his glory (growth in power).

THESE DEFINITIONS OF SPIRITUAL GIFTS ARE NOT *THE* TRUTH; THEY ARE JUST INTENDED TO SHED LIGHT ON THE TRUTH.

DEFINITION

For each of the 30 gifts, you will find a definition reflecting the understanding of the gifts upon which the questions of the *Three-Color Gift Test* have been built. It is important that you read these definitions carefully since interpretation of the individual gifts differs widely from one Christian group to another. Don't be troubled if your own understanding of some gifts differs from the definitions provided here. It is not necessary that you accept my definition in order to discover and apply your spiritual gift. Nor are these definitions *the* truth; they are just intended to shed light on the truth. Much of what is shared here stems from the understanding of spiritual gifts that C. Peter Wagner offers in his excellent book *Your Spiritual Gifts Can Help Your Church Grow* (Regal Books).

BIBLE REFERENCES

The Scripture passages in this section will help you gain further insights into your gifts, using biblical examples. At the same time, these texts offer a basis for discussion in small groups. Please note, however, that not every passage speaks directly of a spiritual gift. At times they refer to the "universal responsibility" (page 52). Still, all of these texts deal with topics that relate to the gift under consideration. The passages in **bold print** are particularly appropriate for Bible study in a small group. You may want to have a series of studies based upon the gifts discovered in the group so that members can encourage one another to use their gifts.

POSSIBLE TASKS

In this section you will find a list of tasks that suggests ways to apply the gift under consideration. When considering this list, note that often more than one gift is necessary to complete a certain task. If you are still uncertain if you have a specific gift—this is often the case with latent gifts—then it is wise, for a limited period of time, to accept tasks of this kind so that you have a chance to experiment in this area. If you have already discovered that you have a certain gift (a manifest gift), then use the list to ascertain whether there is an appropriate task in which you can utilize your gift. Please add any tasks to the list that you feel may require people who have the gift under discussion. The list contains examples intended to stimulate your own creativity; it is not exhaustive.

DANGERS

There are certain dangers associated with each gift. Awareness of them will not make you immune to pitfalls, but you can take measures to avoid them. For this reason, I recommend that you read this section very carefully, especially with regard to your manifest gifts. Better yet, read it again and again.

THERE ARE CERTAIN DANGERS ASSOCIATED WITH EACH GIFT. AWARENESS OF THEM WILL NOT MAKE YOU IMMUNE TO PITFALLS, BUT YOU CAN TAKE MEASURES TO AVOID THEM.

TIPS FOR TRAINING THE GIFTS

These tips are intended primarily for those who have discovered that they have the gift under discussion. At the same time, these tips can prove to be helpful for others as well, enabling them to more effectively practice the corresponding universal responsibility (see page 52).

QUESTIONS

For each of the gifts, I have formulated two questions that are intended to stimulate your thinking on the topic. These questions can be especially helpful if you want to study spiritual gifts in the context of a small group.

CATEGORY 1: THE GREEN AREA

The gifts listed in the green category relate primarily—but not exclusively—to God's revelation in creation. That is the major reason why they can be found outside the Christian context as well. However, they become "spiritual" gifts at the moment we apply them to tasks that serve the kingdom of God.

THE GIFTS LISTED IN THE GREEN CATEGORY RELATE PRIMARILY TO GOD'S REVELATION IN CREATION.

• *One sub-category of these gifts relates to the **development of life-giving environments** (for instance, through social service to the underprivileged in society, reflecting God's love for them):*

❏ *Giving*

❏ *Hospitality*

❏ *Mercy*

❏ *Voluntary poverty*

• *A second sub-category helps people **develop ideas and systems** that will benefit the kingdom of God:*

❏ *Knowledge*

❏ *Organization*

❏ *Wisdom*

• *A third sub-category enables us to **develop things of purpose and beauty:***

❏ *Artistic creativity*

❏ *Craftsmanship*

❏ *Music*

THE GIFT OF ARTISTIC CREATIVITY

The gift of artistic creativity appears in a great variety of forms such as dance, sculpture, pottery, pantomime, music, composition, and writing. In contrast to the gift of craftsmanship, the gift of artistic creativity focuses on the *creative* element. Whatever the medium used, it is only a means to the end of expressing a specific idea or feeling.

SCRIPTURE REFERENCES

Exodus 31:1–11, 2 Samuel 6:12–16, 1 Kings 7:14

POSSIBLE TASKS

Layout of church publications, choreography, developing public relations materials, web development, new forms of worship, arts and crafts group, drama, video projects, interior decoration, lyrics, musical composition ...

THIS GIFT ENABLES YOU TO USE ARTISTIC EXPRESSION FOR THE EDIFICATION OF OTHERS.

DANGERS

- Some people are so taken up with the "great artists" and their "immortal accomplishments" that they don't trust themselves to employ their own creative genius.

- Some people who have this gift are extremely sensitive and are not able to deal with criticism.

- Some artistic productions that Christians create are more for the purpose of self-exposure than for aiding the kingdom of God.

TIPS FOR TRAINING THIS GIFT

- If you have identified this as one of your gifts, you should ask yourself if your life calling might be found in the use of some creative art form.

- Seek out contact with other creative individuals (both Christian and non-Christian).

- Invest time in the trade (skill/handiwork) side of the artistic process.

QUESTIONS

- Can you recall examples of how your own faith has been enriched through artistic creativity (painting, music, prose, etc.)?

- To what extent is it possible to exercise this gift in your own church?

THE GIFT OF CRAFTSMANSHIP

The gift of craftsmanship can be used in a multitude of ways (gardening, building, car repair, as well as tasks that might be traditionally seen as "female" tasks, such as sewing, etc.). Observe, however, that not everyone who is skillful with his or her hands has this gift. People who don't have this gift might love crafts, but they don't experience the overwhelming joy that arises from exercising their gift for the benefit of others. This joy of ministering to others, however, is characteristic of those who have the spiritual gift of craftsmanship.

THIS GIFT ENABLES YOU TO USE A TRADE OR CRAFT FOR THE GOOD OF THE BODY OF CHRIST.

SCRIPTURE REFERENCES

Exodus 30:22–31, 2 Kings 12:11–13, 2 Chronicles 34:9–13, Acts 18:3

POSSIBLE TASKS

Building, gardening, helping others with odd jobs in the neighborhood, maintenance, technical team, missions, sewing projects ...

DANGERS

- Some people with this gift suffer from feelings of inferiority because their gifts are not perceived as spiritual.
- Countless Christians with this gift use their skills in their circle of friends and relatives, but not in their church.

TIPS FOR TRAINING THIS GIFT

- A good way to develop your own skill is to "look over the shoulder" of others while they are practicing their trade and to let them teach you.
- If you are already aware of some of your own special trade skills, test your gifting in some other trades, as well.
- Offer your skills to the service of your church. Direct the work of others that don't share your gift or skills.
- Use your gift to help people in your neighborhood.

QUESTIONS

- Should your church exclusively call upon church members with this gift, or should it also contract professionals from outside the church?
- Which Christians do you know with this gift? Do they understand their skill as being a spiritual gift? How are they using it to build up the body of Christ?

THE GIFT OF GIVING

You don't need a special gift to tithe regularly. There are individuals, however, that give a significant percentage beyond their tithe to the kingdom of God. The gift of giving is not to be confused with the gift of voluntary poverty (see page 101), even if these two frequently appear together in one's gift mix.

SCRIPTURE REFERENCES

Luke 3:11, Luke 21:1–4, John 12:3–8, Acts 4:32–37, Acts 20:35, Romans 12:8, **2 Corinthians 8:2–5**

POSSIBLE TASKS

Finance committee member, supporting missionaries, treasurer, full-time financial adviser, tithe coordinator, assisting in crises, supporting special projects ...

THIS GIFT ENABLES YOU TO GIVE MATERIAL THINGS CHEERFULLY AND GENEROUSLY TO OTHERS.

DANGERS

- Some Christians with this gift run the risk of holding back when they face tight situations in their personal finances. This gift's use should not depend on prosperity, however.

- At times God blesses people that have this gift with vast amounts of money. There is danger in thinking that this money should be withheld for one's own personal use.

- Some Christians tend to give their money away to non-profit organizations out of the pure joy of giving, yet without an overall plan. Some structure and long-term planning would compound the value of such donations.

- Some people with this gift believe that giving money toward certain projects is all that they need to do.

TIPS FOR TRAINING THIS GIFT

- Become intimately familiar with the ministries that you support. Get to know the individuals who benefit from your contributions.

- Keep your eyes open for needs that others don't recognize and consciously invest in those ministries. Pay particular attention to projects that would not be possible without your support.

QUESTIONS

- Have you ever experienced God's special blessing as a result of some gift you gave? Did this experience motivate you to give more? If so, how?

- List additional projects that your church could take on if every Christian tithed and every person with the gift of giving (our research indicates that this is approximately 14 percent in most Christian groups) applied this gift.

THE GIFT OF HOSPITALITY

People with the gift of hospitality are usually happier when they have guests than when they don't. Please note that it is not a prerequisite that you possess this gift to maintain an open home and be friendly to visitors. Hospitality is to be exercised by all Christians as one of the universal Christian responsibilities (see page 52). Those with this gift, however, are able to make their guests really feel at home. Most of them can create this atmosphere even outside their own homes.

THIS GIFT ENABLES YOU TO MAINTAIN AN OPEN HOME, OFFERING FOOD AND LODGING TO GUESTS.

SCRIPTURE REFERENCES

Genesis 18:1–8, Matthew 10:11–14 and 40, Matthew 25:35, Luke 10:38–42, Romans 12:9–13, Titus 1:7–8, 1 Peter 4:9–10, Hebrews 13:1–2, 3 John 5–10

POSSIBLE TASKS

Small group host, caring for the homeless, worship service greeter, ministry to the underprivileged, retreat leadership, church exchanges, hosting guests, preparing accommodations for groups, youth ministry ...

DANGERS

- Some people enjoy exercising this gift to such a degree that family members without this gift suffer from the constant influx of guests.
- Gift projection (see page 87) is common among people with the gift of hospitality. When those with this gift are being hosted by people who don't have this gift, they might feel as if they are being treated in an unfriendly manner. No fault is to be found in the host; it's just that he or she doesn't have the gift of hospitality.

TIPS FOR TRAINING THIS GIFT

- Inform your church that you are willing to accommodate guests whenever the need arises.
- Consider having some group meet in your home. This does not mean that you assume the leadership, but rather that you serve as the host or hostess.

QUESTIONS

- Have you ever been hosted by someone with this gift? Describe how you felt.
- Which of the following gifts do you regard as contributing most to church development: hospitality, tongues, shepherding, or teaching? Explain your answer.

THE GIFT OF KNOWLEDGE

Christians differ in their understanding of the gift of knowledge. Some understand knowledge (and wisdom) to be transrational insight into specific situations. This phenomenon certainly exists, but in this book it is addressed under the gift of prophecy (see page 122). People with the gift of knowledge develop new ideas that are valuable for the kingdom of God. Sixty-six percent of those with the gift of knowledge also have the gift of teaching—a particularly useful gift mix.

SCRIPTURE REFERENCES

Romans 15:14, 1 Corinthians 8:1–2, 1 Corinthians 12:8, 1 Corinthians 13:2 and 8–10, 2 Corinthians 12:7, **Ephesians 3:14–19**

POSSIBLE TASKS

Church growth research, seminar preparation, writing, long-term planning, Bible study, journalism, theological studies, academic work, creative evangelistic outreach ...

THIS GIFT ENABLES YOU TO GENERATE, COLLECT, AND ANALYZE IDEAS WHICH ARE IMPORTANT FOR THE HEALTH OF THE CHURCH.

DANGERS

- For some people, this gift has become an end in itself. They accumulate knowledge for the sake of knowledge, without ever asking about its value for the kingdom of God.
- Some people with this gift have an underdeveloped view of practical ministries. This is particularly true of those who don't have the gift of teaching as a part of their gift mix.
- People with the gift of knowledge run the risk of developing a proud spirit since they are typically more knowledgeable than others.

TIPS FOR TRAINING THIS GIFT

- Spend more time studying the Bible.
- Gather data and facts that are relevant to church development.
- Familiarize yourself with techniques for developing new ideas. Numerous worthwhile books are available in this field.
- Set up an idea file; use it and keep it current.

QUESTIONS

- Whom do you know with the gift of knowledge? Are they using their gift for church development? In what ways?
- Do those with the gift of knowledge derive their insights from natural or supernatural sources? Are both sources valid in the kingdom of God? Explain.

THE GIFT OF MERCY

The gift of mercy can be distinguished from the gift of helps or service in that it typically reaches out to those on the perimeter of society. While people with the gift of counseling minister primarily through loving *words*, those with the gift of mercy seek to meet the needs of others through loving *action*. In many cases, this gift is still undiscovered. Our research indicates that 13 percent of all Christians have the gift of mercy as a part of their gift mix.

THIS GIFT ENABLES YOU TO DEMONSTRATE EMPATHY THROUGH PRACTICAL DEEDS TOWARD THOSE WHO ARE TROUBLED IN MIND, BODY, OR SPIRIT.

SCRIPTURE REFERENCES

Matthew 25:37–40, Mark 9:41, **Luke 10:33–37**, Acts 9:36–42, Romans 12:4–8, James 1:27, James 2:14–17

POSSIBLE TASKS

Counseling sessions, intercessory prayer, ministry to the underprivileged, prison ministry, foreign missions, ministry to single mothers/fathers, ministry to the handicapped, hospital/sick calls, ministry to the chemically dependent ...

DANGERS

- Some people with this gift are so sensitive to injustice that they tend to have an overly negative view of the world.
- Others have the tendency to react to isolated needs too spontaneously, rather than trying to deal with the root cause of the problem.
- Those with the gift of mercy must be careful not to regard people without this gift as unmerciful.

TIPS FOR TRAINING THIS GIFT

- Keep your eyes open for situations in which you can serve needy people.
- The gift of mercy is not limited to a few specific tasks. Regardless of which task you pursue, this gift can enrich your ministry.
- Those with the gift of mercy will increase the efficacy of their ministry by consciously improving their ability to listen. Many people desire nothing more than a conversation partner who will listen out of genuine interest.

QUESTIONS

- What is the difference between the gift of mercy and the corresponding universal responsibility (see page 52)? Consider several situations in which every Christian should practice mercy and several that are particularly for those with the gift of mercy.
- How do people demonstrate that they have this gift? Record several distinctive characteristics.

THE GIFT OF MUSIC

The gift of music doesn't involve composing music or writing lyrics (that ability belongs to artistic creativity), but rather singing and playing music itself. The Old Testament mentions a variety of roles that apply to this gift: instrumentalists (1 Chron. 15:20f; 2 Chron. 29:26), vocalists (1 Chron. 15:19), worship leaders (Neh. 12:46), and choir directors (1 Chron. 15:22).

SCRIPTURE REFERENCES

Deuteronomy 31:14–22, **1 Samuel 16:14–23**, 1 Chronicles 16:41–42, 2 Chronicles 5:12–14, Psalm 150, 1 Corinthians 14:26, Ephesians 5:18–20, Colossians 3:15–17

THIS GIFT ENABLES YOU TO PLAY A MUSICAL INSTRUMENT OR TO USE THEIR VOICE IN SINGING FOR THE GLORY OF GOD AND THE EDIFICATION OF OTHERS.

POSSIBLE TASKS

Worship leader, instrumentalist, music teacher, worship team, street outreach, choir director, choir member, planning worship services, vocal soloist, evangelistic outreach ...

DANGERS

* Some Christians, upon recognizing that they have this gift, think that they don't need to train their musical gift any more since it "comes from God." This can have unpleasant consequences.

* Some musicians are so celebrated by their fans that these "stars" actually assume more authority in a variety of different areas of everyday life than is rightfully deserved.

* Not everyone that has the gift of music makes a good leader of a music group (band, worship team, choir, etc.).

TIPS FOR TRAINING THIS GIFT

* If you really want to develop this gift for the glory of God, take music lessons from a competent teacher.

* Seek to train others in their musical gift and skills—you may even uncover a hidden gift of teaching or leadership.

* Join a group of musicians that performs together.

QUESTIONS

* Is the gift of music a precondition for singing in the choir? Why, or why not?

* Does someone with this gift need to practice more, or less than someone without it? Why?

THE GIFT OF ORGANIZATION

The Greek word for "organizer" can also be translated "steerer," the person on a ship whose job it is to mediate between the captain and the rest of the crew. The difference between the gift of leadership and the gift of organization relates to the difference between the captain and the steerer of a ship. The captain makes the basic decisions regarding the route of the ship, and the helmsman guides the ship safely to her intended destination.

SCRIPTURE REFERENCES

Exodus 18:13–27, 1 Corinthians 12:28

POSSIBLE TASKS

THIS GIFT ENABLES YOU TO UNDERSTAND GOALS FOR SPECIFIC AREAS OF MINISTRY AND TO DRAFT EFFECTIVE PLANS TOWARD REACHING THESE GOALS.

Area superintendent, overseer of ministry area(s), church growth planning, organization of events (such as workshops, conferences, concerts), finances, church celebrations, evangelistic campaigns, coordination of small groups, librarian, leadership in ministry teams, creative worship forms, project planning, preparing church retreats, computer work ...

DANGERS

- Some people with this gift tend to view their contribution as the very essence of church ministry. They see how God blesses their planning and organization and lose the perspective that they are just one tool that God wants to use to build his church.
- People who can only see the practical, organizational side of ministry often function as "brakes" for the visionaries in a church.
- People with this gift must pay particularly close attention to their spiritual life. Experience with the supernatural works of God can help maintain balance in exercising this gift.

TIPS FOR TRAINING THIS GIFT

- Attend management seminars, secular as well as Christian, that will enable you to better apply this gift.
- Consistently use a time-management system that can help you use your time more efficiently.

QUESTIONS

- Which tasks in your church could be carried out more effectively if people with this gift were to get involved?
- What, if anything, stands in the way of delegating these tasks to someone with the gift of organization?

THE GIFT OF VOLUNTARY POVERTY

CHAPTER 5:
30 SPIRITUAL
GIFTS

In our understanding of the gift of voluntary poverty, the word "voluntary" is essential. Not everyone with a modest lifestyle has this gift. Rather, the gift of voluntary poverty is exercised by those who could maintain a higher standard of living but consciously choose not to. Don't confuse this gift with that of "giving." It is true that almost everyone who has the gift of voluntary poverty also has the gift of giving (92 percent have "giving" among their five most prominent manifest gifts). The inverse is not true, however. Our research states that only 15 percent of the Christians with the gift of giving also have the gift of voluntary poverty.

THIS GIFT ENABLES YOU TO DENY THEMSELVES MATERIAL WELL-BEING SO THAT THEY CAN MAINTAIN A STANDARD OF LIVING THAT PARALLELS THE POOR.

SCRIPTURE REFERENCES

Acts 2:44–45, **Acts 4:32–37**, 1 Corinthians 13:3, 2 Corinthians 6:10, Philippians 4:11–13

POSSIBLE TASKS

Foreign missions, ministry to the underprivileged, ministry to the homeless and refugees, community outreach, living in a monastery, pioneer work ...

DANGERS

- People with this gift should exercise it as God intended, but guard against judging other Christians who maintain a higher standard of living.
- Poverty can become an end in itself. This is not the reason God gives this gift. It is given to achieve specific goals. Ask yourself if these goals can truly be achieved at a reduced standard of living.

TIPS FOR TRAINING THIS GIFT

- Spend several days or weeks in a monastery (or retreat center or camp) where strict regulations regarding material possessions are followed.
- Schedule times in which you lower your standard of living, reducing it to a true level of poverty in your society.
- If you live in the western world, visit third-world countries and live in close fellowship with the people.

QUESTIONS

- Reflect on the life of someone like Mother Teresa. Do you think that this lifestyle is a great personal sacrifice for that person? Or do you think that perhaps he or she is happier living that way?
- Should every Christian lead a simple lifestyle, or only those who have this gift?

The gift of wisdom

The gift of wisdom is to be distinguished from the gift of knowledge. Those with the gift of knowledge treat spiritual matters like a medical researcher who seeks to gain insight into physiology, genetics, or the effect of a vaccine through his or her lab work. Those with the gift of wisdom, on the other hand, can be compared to a physician who offers a diagnosis and applies the medical research to each individual case. Caution: Some Christians refer to a "word of wisdom" when they really mean a prophetic utterance (see page 122).

This gift enables you to help others apply existing knowledge to specific situations.

Scripture references

1 Kings 3:5–28, 1 Corinthians 12:7–8, James 3:13–18

Possible tasks

Counseling, conflict resolution, prayer team, career consulting, training courses, gift consulting, seminars, coaching, online forums, church consulting ...

Dangers

* Since the advice of those with the gift of wisdom is eagerly sought by others, there is a danger that they will offer answers in situations where they don't have anything helpful to say. It is possible for them to be elevated to the status of a "guru" whose advice is followed blindly.

* People with this gift are able to anticipate the consequences of certain decisions much better than are others. Therefore, they must guard against browbeating or patronizing others in their charge. It is important for them to allow those under their influence enough freedom to experiment and fail from time to time.

Tips for training this gift

* Work with concrete case studies that will help you learn to relate universal principles to various situations.

* Develop techniques for posing the right questions. It is usually better to ask questions, so that others come up with the solution on their own, than to provide the answers yourself.

Questions

* When have you personally benefited from people that have this gift? Record the details of this experience.

* Would it be valuable for your church to seek out a church consultant? Write down the advantages and disadvantages.

CATEGORY 2: THE RED AREA

The gifts listed in the red category relate to proclaiming the gospel and helping people grow in their knowledge of Christ. That is the major reason why you will find in this category those gifts that enable us to fulfill various leadership roles in the church.

THE GIFTS LISTED IN THE RED CATEGORY RELATE TO PROCLAIMING THE GOSPEL AND HELPING PEOPLE GROW IN THEIR KNOWLEDGE OF CHRIST.

• One sub-category of these gifts quite obviously relates to **sharing the Good News**:

❏ *Evangelism*

❏ *Missionary*

• A second sub-category encompasses various leadership gifts that enable people **sharing the way forward**:

❏ *Apostle*

❏ *Counseling*

❏ *Leadership*

❏ *Shepherding*

❏ *Teaching*

• A third sub-category is focused on **sharing the load** of others (often leaders) so that they can better pursue their tasks:

❏ *Helps*

❏ *Service*

❏ *Singleness*

THE GIFT OF APOSTLE

The gift of apostle is by no means limited to the original twelve apostles. The New Testament offers examples of other men and women in apostolic ministry. An apostle's responsibility typically extends beyond his or her own local church. Their authority is independent of any office they may hold. People with this gift distinguish themselves through their farsighted perspective.

SCRIPTURE REFERENCES

Matthew 10:2–15, John 13:12–17, Acts 8:14–25, Acts 14:14–15, Acts 15:1–6, Romans 16:7, **1 Corinthians 12:28–29**, 2 Corinthians 12:12, Galatians 1:1, Ephesians 4:11

THIS GIFT ENABLES YOU TO BE RECOGNIZED AS SPIRITUAL LEADERS BY A VARIETY OF CHURCHES.

POSSIBLE TASKS

Church planting, church consulting, long-term planning, regional/denominational responsibilities, interdenominational work, foreign missions ...

DANGERS

- Some people with this gift lack spiritual correction. For this reason, it is critical for them to be involved in a group or fellowship in which they exercise no leadership function.
- Not everyone with an apostolic gift has the gifts of leadership and organization. This can lead to a lack of structure in their ministry.
- Some people with the apostolic gift have the role of "guru" imposed upon them. People with this gift must honestly and openly admit that they don't have the answers to each and every question. They must recognize their own limitations as human beings.
- Individuals that are in the spotlight must guard themselves from the age-old temptations of money, sex, and power.

TIPS FOR TRAINING THIS GIFT

- The standards that the Bible provides for "leaders" (1 Tim. 3:1–7; 5:17–22) apply all the more to Christians in apostolic ministry.
- If you have discovered that you have this gift, seek out other people with the same gift and spend time with them so that you can learn from one another.
- People with this gift are wise to remain flexible in terms of their place of residence.

QUESTIONS

- Does each regional or national church leader (e.g., bishop, superintendent, etc.) have to have an apostolic gift? Why, or why not?
- In your opinion, do the regional leaders of your church have an apostolic gift? Explain.

THE GIFT OF COUNSELING

T he gift of counseling tries to combine the two dimensions of the Greek word *parakaleo* which can mean both "admonition" and "encouragement." This gift is different from the gift of shepherding in that the ministry of counseling doesn't require a long-term relationship with the people who receive the ministry. Those with this gift only use it for a limited time period while seeking the personal and spiritual well-being of another. Then they apply this gift in a different situation with a different person. It's interesting to note that 41 percent of Christians who have this gift also have the gift of hospitality.

THIS GIFT ENABLES YOU TO SERVE OTHERS THROUGH COMFORT, ADMONITION, AND ENCOURAGEMENT, SO THAT THEY EXPERIENCE HELP AND HEALING.

SCRIPTURE REFERENCES

John 4:1–42, Acts 14:21–22, Romans 12:6–8, 2 Corinthians 1:3–7, 1 Thessalonians 2:11, **1 Thessalonians 5:14**, 1 Timothy 5:1

POSSIBLE TASKS

Integrating new Christians, hospital ministry, counseling team, small group ministry, gift consulting, prayer team, challenging passive Christians, substance abuse counseling, ministry to the underprivileged, family counseling, seniors ministry, telephone counseling, internet forums, supervision, prison ministry, hospice ministry ...

DANGERS

- Some people with this gift take on too many responsibilities, and their personal (and spiritual) lives suffer.
- Some people who can identify with and show sympathy toward others lack the necessary directness and firmness to deal with the root problems.

TIPS FOR TRAINING THIS GIFT

- Study the Psalms and observe the varying moods of people who sought to walk with God. Consider how you can best apply the Psalms to encourage those who are facing similar situations.
- Reflect on the book of Job. What does it teach about how you should and should *not* interact with those who are suffering?
- Register for courses that give you a basic foundation in psychology.
- Be sure that you have a personal counselor yourself.

QUESTIONS

- Does every Christian who wants to counsel need training in psychology? Why, or why not?
- Which gifts best complement the gift of counseling?

THE GIFT OF EVANGELISM

THIS GIFT ENABLES YOU TO COMMUNICATE THE GOSPEL TO NON-CHRISTIANS IN A MANNER CONDUCIVE TO LEADING THEM TO FAITH.

Our research confirmed the thesis held by C. Peter Wagner that exactly 10 percent of the Christians in each local congregation have the gift of evangelism. Christians who discover this gift should be given enough time to exercise it and, in most cases, should be released from other tasks.

SCRIPTURE REFERENCES

Acts 8:5–6, **Acts 8:26–40**, Acts 14:13–21, Romans 10:14–15, Ephesians 4:11

POSSIBLE TASKS

Preaching, open houses, visitation ministry, counseling, radio ministry, Internet forums, foreign missions, church planting team, ministry to the underprivileged, evangelistic home groups, music or band ministry, children's evangelism, ministry to internationals ...

DANGERS

- Some people with this gift give the impression of a sales person seeking to peddle their wares. In their evangelistic zeal, they can put undue pressure on those with whom they are speaking.
- Some evangelists are so preoccupied with "decisions for Christ" that the process of integrating new believers into a community of Christians is neglected.

TIPS FOR TRAINING THIS GIFT

- Join a group that is involved in regular evangelistic outreach. If there is no such group in your church, start one yourself. Be sure to single out others with the gift of evangelism and invite them to join you.
- Adopt an existing evangelistic program.
- Work together with others who have this gift to a greater extent, and observe how they use their gift. Be sure to ask why they acted in a particular way, whenever you are uncertain.
- Assume the leadership of some evangelistic outreach that will challenge you to grow in your area of gifting.

QUESTIONS

- As you reflect on how you came to faith, which person(s) had the greatest influence on your decision? Why?
- Do you think that they had the gift of evangelism? What makes you think so?

THE GIFT OF HELPS

The gift of helps, like the gift of mercy, focuses on individuals. In contrast to the gift of mercy, however, this gift is not so much intended for the benefit of the underprivileged. Rather, it is more commonly used to lighten the work load of other Christians (most frequently leaders), allowing them more time to exercise their own gifts. The gift of helps should also be distinguished from the gift of service. *Service* aims at serving organizations; *helps* aims at helping individuals.

SCRIPTURE REFERENCES

Exodus 18:21–22, Numbers 11:16–17, **Luke 10:38–42**, Romans 16:1–2, 1 Corinthians 12:28

POSSIBLE TASKS

Telephone ministry, supporting leaders, secretarial help, helping families move into new homes, web support, custodial service ...

DANGERS

THIS GIFT ENABLES YOU TO PLACE THEIR OWN GIFTS AT THE DISPOSAL OF OTHERS, THUS RELEASING THEM TO CONCENTRATE MORE ON THEIR MINISTRY.

- Some people suffer from a social disorder referred to as "helper's syndrome." Such people would likely complete the *Three-Color Gift Test* in such a manner that "helps" appears as one of their manifest spiritual gifts, but this would be a faulty result.
- On the other hand, some people who are exemplary in their practice of the gift of helps may be erroneously suspected as having "helper's syndrome."
- There is a general danger that people with the gift of helps exaggerate their concern for others to such an extent that those in need actually become co-dependent.

TIPS FOR TRAINING THIS GIFT

- Should you discover that you have this gift, ask the leader(s) of your church, "What can I do for you to help lighten your load?"
- The gift of helps can be expressed through diverse activities, including: typing, laundry, painting, filing, correspondence, speech-writing, etc. Try to concentrate your abilities in an area that is particularly needed. Pay special attention to areas where overtaxed leaders need your assistance.

QUESTIONS

- In what way could the leaders of your church be aided if the gift of helps was consistently exercised?
- According to our research, 13 percent of all Christians have the gift of helps. Do the Christians in your church who have this gift know that it is a spiritual gift?

THE GIFT OF LEADERSHIP

The trademark of a leader is that others follow him or her of their own free will rather than by coercion. People with this gift usually don't have to stress their "leadership authority" (in most cases, this is an indication that one does not have this gift). It is interesting that 68 percent of all Christians with this gift also have the gift of organization.

SCRIPTURE REFERENCES

Exodus 18:13–27, Romans 12:8, 1 Thessalonians 5:12–13, **1 Timothy 3:1–7,** 1 Timothy 5:17–22

THIS GIFT ENABLES YOU TO SET GOALS FOR THE CHURCH AND TO COMMUNICATE THEM IN SUCH A WAY THAT OTHERS VOLUNTEER TO ACHIEVE THEM.

POSSIBLE TASKS

Pastor, elder, worship service leader, department leader, long-term planning, church planting, pioneer work, initiating new ministries ...

DANGERS

• A constant danger to all leaders is spiritual isolation. Many leaders don't have anyone who can see them as they really are and hold them accountable.

• Any public figure who spends much of his or her time in the limelight will experience temptation in the areas of money, sex, and power.

• Some leaders find it difficult to remain humble. The New Testament explicitly admonishes leaders to be humble (cf. 1 Peter 5:5–6).

TIPS FOR TRAINING THIS GIFT

• Study the biblical statements regarding spiritual leadership. The gift of leadership is only one of many criteria for Christian leaders.

• Study biblical figures such as Abraham, Joshua, Moses, David, Elijah, Elisha, Samuel, and Paul.

• Biographical studies of great leaders can prove helpful for learning more about principles of leadership.

• Focus your ministry on finding and developing new leaders.

QUESTIONS

• Consider those in your church in leadership positions. Do these individuals have the gift of leadership? How can you tell?

• Reflect on others you may know who possess this gift. Which gifts are frequently combined with the gift of leadership?

THE GIFT OF MISSIONARY

Christians with the gift of missionary enjoy leaving their own culture in order to establish a new home and ministry in a foreign culture. This gift can be exercised in a foreign country, as well as within a different social group in their home country. The gift of missionary should not be confused with the gift of evangelism (see page 106). Only 8 percent of all Christians whom God has blessed with the gift of missionary have the gift of evangelism too.

SCRIPTURE REFERENCES

Acts 9:13–17, Acts 14:21–28, **1 Corinthians 9:19–23**, Galatians 1:15–17, Galatians 2:7–14, Ephesians 3:6–8

POSSIBLE TASKS

Ministry to the underprivileged, ministry to internationals, foreign missions, church planting, intercultural dialogue, ministry to specific target groups ...

THIS GIFT ENABLES YOU TO UTILIZE THEIR OTHER GIFTS IN A SECOND CULTURE.

DANGERS

- Some Christians with this gift are so accommodating that they either water down the gospel message or fail to communicate it. This is particularly true for those who don't have the gift of evangelism in their gift mix.

- More than with the other gifts, practicing this gift has implications for all areas of one's life, including family and occupation. Therefore, Christians with this gift should carefully evaluate to which long-term duties they commit themselves.

TIPS FOR TRAINING THIS GIFT

- Use trips abroad to interact with people from foreign cultures and, if possible, to share in their lifestyle for some time.

- Make friends with internationals in your area and invite them into your home.

- Look for opportunities to use your gift in countries or areas that need missionaries. In light of the fact that more than 30 percent of the world's population is still "unreached," everyone with this gift should seriously consider whether God is calling him or her to one of those mission fields.

QUESTIONS

- What exactly is the difference between the gift of missionary and the gift of evangelism?

- "Everyone should become a foreign missionary if God has not called them to stay home." What do you think of this statement?

THE GIFT OF SERVICE

I n contrast to the gift of helps, which usually focuses on assisting an individual (very often a leader), the gift of service is directed toward groups and organizations. People with the gift of service typically have an eye for things that need to be done, and they are willing to fulfill that need themselves. Every group benefits from Christians who exercise this gift. The gifts of service and helps are among the gifts that are most frequently paired together. According to our research, 81 percent of Christians who have the gift of service also have the gift of helps.

THIS GIFT ENABLES YOU TO RECOGNIZE WHERE THEIR PARTICIPATION IS NEEDED AND TO MAKE SURE THAT THE MOST URGENT JOBS GET DONE.

SCRIPTURE REFERENCES

Luke 10:38–42, **Luke 22:24–27**, Acts 6:1–7, Romans 12:6–7, 1 Timothy 3:8–13

POSSIBLE TASKS

Odd jobs, gardening, caring for guests, cooking and baking, maintenance, typing/computer work, tape ministry, baby-sitting, emergency ministry ...

DANGERS

- Some people with this gift have a propensity to assume the ministry tasks of others, which makes these people co-dependent.
- Those with this gift are sometimes rather shamelessly taken advantage of by others.
- People with an eye for spotting ministry opportunities and actively seeking to meet existing needs often judge those who are not able to do this—a classic case of gift projection (see page 87).

TIPS FOR TRAINING THIS GIFT

- Serving can take many different forms. Consciously strengthen your abilities in the areas in which you are involved. For example, if you apply your gift in secretarial tasks, expand your potential for exercising this gift by learning new computer and web development skills.
- If you have the gift of service, inform your church leadership. Make them aware of the ministries in which you are prepared to become involved. Don't grow impatient if there is no immediate response to your offer.

QUESTIONS

- Which tasks in your church could be carried out more successfully if those with the gift of service were actively applying their gifts?
- What obstacles in your church are hindering those with this gift from consistently exercising it?

THE GIFT OF SHEPHERDING

The gift of shepherding—in contrast to the gift of counseling—involves a long-term commitment to a group of people. Contrary to widespread opinion, this gift is not necessary for a pastor of a local church. Our research indicates that the gift of shepherding is relatively widespread, appearing in 12 percent of the gift mixes of all Christians. Interestingly, 43 percent of all Christians with the gift of shepherding also have the gift of teaching.

SCRIPTURE REFERENCES

John 10:1–15, Acts 20:28–31, Ephesians 4:11, 1 Thessalonians 5:12–13, 1 Timothy 4:11–16, Hebrews 13:7,17 and 20–21, 1 Peter 5:1–5

POSSIBLE TASKS

Gift consultant, children's church, small group leader, youth ministry, assimilating new Christians, informal gatherings, training programs ...

THIS GIFT ENABLES YOU TO ASSUME LONG-TERM, PERSONAL RESPONSIBILITY FOR THE SPIRITUAL WELL-BEING OF A GROUP OF PEOPLE.

DANGERS

- Sometimes people with this gift lead groups that function well internally, but have difficulty integrating newcomers.
- Pastors with this gift will have difficulty leading a church of more than 150–200 believers. They want to maintain a close relationship with every single person, but this kind of relationship is simply not possible with more than 150–200 people.

TIPS FOR TRAINING THIS GIFT

- An important task for those with the gift of shepherding is to help others discover and to put into practice their spiritual gifts.
- If you lead a group of people, look for ways to multiply the group.
- Take advantage of training opportunities in counseling, since the gift of counseling and shepherding are closely related.

QUESTIONS

- Twelve percent of all Christians have this gift. Why do you think this gift is so prevalent?
- Leading small groups is an ideal ministry for those who have this gift. In your opinion, do the small group leaders of your church have this gift? Are there individuals in your church with the gift of shepherding who haven't yet found any relevant tasks in which they can exercise this gift?

THE GIFT OF SINGLENESS

THIS GIFT ENABLES YOU TO LIVE HAPPILY AS SINGLES WHILE CONTRIBUTING MORE EFFECTIVELY TO THE KINGDOM OF GOD.

The gift of missionary and the gift of singleness are two gifts which, in contrast to all other gifts, can only be exercised meaningfully in combination with other gifts. In other words, they cannot stand on their own. Anyone with the gift of singleness will likely be able to exercise his or her other gifts more effectively. Those with this gift are happier in their singleness than they would be if they were married.

SCRIPTURE REFERENCES

Matthew 19:10–12, 1 Corinthians 7:7–8, **1 Corinthians 7:32–35**, 1 Timothy 4:1–5

POSSIBLE TASKS

Since the gift of singleness is intended to make other gifts more effective, it is theoretically possible to combine any task with it. However, those involved in foreign missions, church planting, and similar pioneer work may particularly profit from this gift since a great degree of flexibility is required in these ministries. This kind of flexibility is often difficult to harmonize with family concerns.

DANGERS

- Some people who have the gift of singleness marry as a concession to social pressure, which is often felt the strongest within Christian circles. Anyone with this gift should resist this kind of pressure.
- Some people who are unable to build relationships as a result of a psychological or social disorder, tend to complete the *Three-Color Gift Test* in such a way that singleness—erroneously—appears as one of their gifts.
- Other people are models in practicing their singleness, yet they still haven't recognized it as a spiritual gift. The result is that they are troubled with the thought that something is out of order in their lives.
- Those with the gift of singleness are not immune to sexual temptation. They should not overestimate their abilities in this area.

TIPS FOR TRAINING THIS GIFT

- Tell yourself every day, "Singleness is my spiritual gift." This recognition alone has helped many people to become more effective in their ministry.
- Get together with other people with the gift of singleness and share your experiences.

QUESTIONS

- Do you regard the oath of celibacy in the Roman Catholic Church to be an appropriate means of exercising the gift of singleness? Why, or why not?
- Is it necessary to have a specific spiritual gift to get married?

THE GIFT OF TEACHING

C haracteristic of the gift of teaching is the fact that others actually learn. Just knowing a lot (which may be an indication of the gift of knowledge, see page 97), should not be confused with the gift of teaching. Those with the gift of teaching are focused on the questions and concerns of their audience, and manage to impart their knowledge in an interesting and stimulating manner.

SCRIPTURE REFERENCES

Acts 18:24–28, Romans 12:6–7, 1 Corinthians 12:28–29, Ephesians 4:11–14, **James 3:1**

POSSIBLE TASKS

Small group ministry, seminars, training courses, Bible studies, new members/baptism class, online work, church growth training ...

THIS GIFT ENABLES YOU TO COMMUNICATE TRUTH IN A MANNER THAT ENABLES OTHERS TO LEARN AND CONTRIBUTES TO THE HEALTH OF THE CHURCH.

DANGERS

- According to Scripture, teachers will be judged "more strictly" than others (James 3:1). Those who have discovered this gift should search for means of exercising it with a high degree of responsibility.

- Some teachers can communicate certain truths extremely well, but don't practice what they teach.

TIPS FOR TRAINING THIS GIFT

- Consciously schedule time for study and preparation. Don't assume that because you have this gift, you need less preparation time than others.

- Always maintain the attitude of a "learner." There are few people more boring than those who always say the same things without expanding their thinking.

- Learn the basics of Bible study methods and exegesis. Focus especially on the practical application for your audience.

- Read books covering topics such as communication and rhetoric. Learn to use visual aids to your benefit, for instance, PowerPoint, flip charts, computer simulations, etc.

QUESTIONS

- Why do you suppose the Bible suggests that teachers will be subject to more severe judgement?

- Reflect on the various teachers, professors, and pastors that you know. Which of them has the gift of teaching? How can you see this gift in their lives?

CATEGORY 3:
THE BLUE AREA

The gifts listed in the blue category demonstrate the power of God. Many of them transcend the limits of rationality in order to show God's power over nature and to minister to people whose needs could not be met by conventional means.

• One sub-category of the blue gifts is focused on **renewing trust in God**. While this trait should characterize every believer, people with these gifts demonstrate this quality to a far higher degree:

THE GIFTS IN THE BLUE CATEGORY DEMONSTRATE THE POWER OF GOD THAT TRANSCENDS OUR RATIONALITY.

❐ Faith

❐ Prayer

❐ Suffering

• A second sub-category **renews people's connection with God** and enables them to share messages from God:

❐ Discernment

❐ Interpretation

❐ Prophecy

❐ Tongues

• A third sub-category **renews people through the power of God** in a way that transcends rational understanding:

❐ Deliverance

❐ Healing

❐ Miracles

THE GIFT OF DELIVERANCE

Power over evil spirits is given to each Christian (Mark 16:15–18). Yet, experience indicates that God uses some Christians more than others in exercising this power. The gift of discernment (see page 116) should be present in any group that is involved in a ministry of deliverance.

SCRIPTURE REFERENCES

Matthew 10:1, Matthew 12:28–29 and 43–45, Mark 5:1–20, Mark 9:28–29, Mark 16:17, **Luke 10:17–20**, Acts 8:5–8, Acts 16:16–18, Acts 19:13–16

THIS GIFT ENABLES YOU TO HELP PEOPLE SUFFERING FROM DEMONIC OPPRESSION EXPERIENCE DELIVERANCE.

POSSIBLE TASKS

Exorcism, ministry to the underprivileged, prayer team ministry, counseling, evangelistic events, foreign missions ...

DANGERS

- There are Christians with this gift who tend to identify evil spirits as the cause of problems that have completely different sources. This can lead to great confusion for those who are earnestly seeking solutions to their troubles.

- For those people who are regularly involved in this ministry, there is an inherent danger of giving too much importance to the demonic dimension.

TIPS FOR TRAINING THIS GIFT

- Carry out this ministry together with others who are experienced in casting out demons. After ministering together, ask why they acted as they did and request some feed-back on your own involvement.

- Ask God to endow you with the gift of discernment, which is very important for dealing in a responsible way with demonically-oppressed people.

- Maintain the protection of a Christian fellowship that will pray for you regularly. Use the protection of spiritual warfare as described in Ephesians 6:11–17.

QUESTIONS

- Are you convinced that there are demons active in the world today? How would you define a "demon?" Have you ever experienced the influence of demons in any perceptible manner?

- Is it possible for Christians to be oppressed by demons? Why, or why not?

THE GIFT OF DISCERNMENT

THIS GIFT ENABLES YOU TO KNOW FOR SURE WHETHER A GIVEN BEHAVIOR ORIGINATES FROM A DIVINE, HUMAN, OR SATANIC SOURCE.

The gift of discernment is part of God's providential protection against error. It can express itself on a natural level by enabling Christians to distinguish between truth and deception. It can also provide them with insight into the deepest sources of truth and deception, thus entering into the supernatural realm.

SCRIPTURE REFERENCES

Matthew 16:22–23, Acts 5:1–10, Acts 8:18–24, Acts 13:6–12, **Acts 16:16–22**, 1 Corinthians 12:10, 1 Thessalonians 5:19–22, 1 John 4:1–6

POSSIBLE TASKS

Public relations, counseling, deliverance ministry, ministry to the underprivileged, church board member, evangelistic campaigns, preaching, prayer team ministry, long-term planning, interreligious dialogue ...

DANGERS

• Some people who have this gift tend to be unloving and coldhearted in exercising it. Others do not apply the gift to the edification of the church. They have difficulty confronting others and therefore, choose to remain silent.

• Even those who have this gift can be wrong at times. Anyone who acts as if he or she is infallible is not suitable for this ministry.

• Some people with this gift tend to develop a "spirit of criticism" that can cause them to criticize almost everything.

TIPS FOR TRAINING THIS GIFT

• A solid biblical foundation is a prerequisite for a responsible exercise of this gift.

• Make sure that the practice of this gift is confirmed by others.

• Exercise this gift with love. Ask God to bless you with an extra amount of sensitivity.

QUESTIONS

• Suppose someone were to stand up in your worship service and exclaim, "This part of the sermon is inconsistent with the Word of God!" What would happen?

• How and when is this gift used in your church?

THE GIFT OF FAITH

While it is every Christian's calling to trust the Lord in all of life's challenges, God has blessed some people with a special gift of faith. These individuals literally have a "mountain-moving" faith (Matt. 17:20). They don't shy away from uncertainties and risks when they are convinced of the will of God. People with this gift are often visionaries who initiate new developments.

SCRIPTURE REFERENCES

Matthew 8:5–13, Matthew 17:20b, Matthew 21:18–22, **Romans 4:18–21**, 1 Corinthians 12:9, James 1:5–8

POSSIBLE TASKS

Prayer group leader, church board member, long-term planning, church planting, creative ideas team, denominational leadership, church leadership for missions, pioneer work, initiating new ministries, evangelism ...

THIS GIFT ENABLES YOU TO DISCERN, WITH AN UNUSUAL DEGREE OF CONFIDENCE, THE WILL OF GOD FOR THE FUTURE DEVELOPMENT OF MINISTRY.

DANGERS

*   Those with the gift of faith tend toward gift projection (see page 87). Sometimes they judge others as being "small-thinking."

*   Some people with this gift are not able to admit when their goals or vision have not been realized.

*   Since those with the gift of faith often demonstrate a unique assurance that they are in harmony with the will of God, they sometimes interpret criticism of themselves as criticism of God.

TIPS FOR TRAINING THIS GIFT

*   Record specific answers to prayer as a means of growing in your faith.

*   Learn to respond more positively to criticism.

*   Seek out fellowship with those who also have this gift.

*   Admit when you make an error in judgment, and don't exaggerate.

*   Learn from Bible characters such as Abraham, Joseph, Moses, Elijah, Elisha, and Samuel, who also had this gift.

QUESTIONS

*   Whom do you know with this gift? Do they motivate or frustrate you when you are around them?

*   Those with this gift are often considered "dreamers." Would you say it is advisable to appoint such people to leadership positions? Do some of the leaders of your church have this gift?

THE GIFT OF HEALING

THIS GIFT ENABLES YOU TO SERVE AS GOD'S INSTRUMENTS FOR RESTORING THE HEALTH OF OTHERS WITHOUT THE AID OF MEDICAL TOOLS.

While the New Testament admonishes all believers to pray for the sick (Mark 16:18), God has given some people the special gift of healing. It is always God who does the healing; men and women can only pray to this end. The gift of healing can appear in different variations (see page 50). There are certain individuals, for example, that God uses to heal wounds of the soul ("inner healing").

SCRIPTURE REFERENCES

Mark 2:1–12, Mark 8:22–26, Mark 16:17–18, John 9:1–12, John 14:12–14, Acts 3:1–8, Acts 14:8–15, Acts 28:8–9, 1 Corinthians 12:9 and 28–30, **James 5:14–15**

POSSIBLE TASKS

Counseling, prayer team, evangelism team, visiting the sick ...

DANGERS

• Some Christians believe that when someone is not healed after much prayer, it must be due to a lack of faith. This misconception can send people into a spiritual tailspin.

• God uses both medical treatment and healing by prayer. We should never treat the two as alternatives.

TIPS FOR TRAINING THIS GIFT

• If you don't see God heal someone through the exercise of your gift over a long period of time, you needn't become discouraged. It is not uncommon for a breakthrough to occur only after months of prayer.

• Whenever possible, pray with a team for the healing of others. Reflect together on what you have experienced.

• Record in a notebook your experiences of praying for the sick. This will help you to identify certain patterns reflecting how, when, and why God chooses to intervene.

QUESTIONS

• Are you aware of any supernatural healings in your own circle of friends and acquaintances? Did you react with joy or skepticism at the news of healing?

• Are you aware of cases in which certain persons were not healed, despite long periods of prayer? How do you interpret these situations?

THE GIFT OF INTERPRETATION

Some Christians with the gift of interpretation interpret the messages that another person has given in tongues; some interpret their own statements. According to the New Testament, a public message in tongues is meaningless without the corresponding interpretation (1 Cor. 14:27–28). Our research indicates that 82 percent of all Christians with this gift also have the gift of prophecy.

SCRIPTURE REFERENCES

1 Corinthians 12:10, 1 Corinthians 12:27–31, 1 Corinthians 14:1–5, 1 Corinthians 14:12–19, **1 Corinthians 14:26–28**

POSSIBLE TASKS

Prayer groups, worship service team, spiritual warfare …

DANGERS

- Since this gift is often exercised in a context in which people are extremely receptive toward this ministry, there is the danger that an irresponsible interpretation might cause great harm.
- This gift is not to be used in large gatherings if it has not first been confirmed in smaller circles.

TIPS FOR TRAINING THIS GIFT

- Whenever a person exercises the gift of tongues in public, ask God to reveal to you the proper interpretation.
- If this gift is not used in your church, take the opportunity to visit events at which you may have the opportunity to exercise this gift.
- Speak with another Christian who has more experience with this gift and ask if his or her interpretation would have matched yours.

QUESTIONS

- According to the Bible, must an interpretation be provided every time someone speaks in tongues?
- In your opinion, why is it that this gift is used in some churches and not in others?

THIS GIFT ENABLES YOU TO MAKE KNOWN IN A COMMONLY UNDERSTOOD LANGUAGE A MESSAGE ORIGINALLY COMMUNICATED IN TONGUES.

THE GIFT OF MIRACLES

THIS GIFT ENABLES YOU TO SERVE AS HUMAN INSTRU- MENTS THROUGH WHOM GOD PER- FORMS POWERFUL ACTS THAT, IN THE EYES OF THE OBSERVER, SUR- PASS NATURAL LAWS.

Whereas the gift of healing might not necessarily break physical laws (the focus is just that healing takes place without the use of medical tools), it is characteristic of the gift of miracles that laws of nature are—in the eyes of the observer—surpassed. Wherever God works a miracle through this gift, it is his goal to communicate a specific message to his people.

SCRIPTURE REFERENCES

Exodus 14:21–31, 1 Kings 18:21–40, Matthew 14:28–33, Matthew 24:23–24, Luke 10:17–20, John 14:2–14, Acts 9:36–42, Acts 19:11, **Acts 20:9–12**, Romans 15:18–19, 1 Corinthians 12:10 and 28, 2 Corinthians 12:12

POSSIBLE TASKS

Foreign missions, spiritual warfare, prayer ministry ...

DANGERS

• Some people abuse this gift by putting on a show that exalts themselves rather than glorifying God.

• In other Christian circles, this gift is viewed so skeptically that those who have it dare not exercise, or even talk about it.

• Some people with this gift tend to exaggerate in retelling their experiences.

TIPS FOR TRAINING THIS GIFT

• Westerners should build relationships with people in non-western cultures. Through these contacts they can learn a lot about the practical relevance of this gift, especially with regard to church development.

• Anyone intending to report miracles that have occurred should carefully consider what form these reports will take. The more precise and sober the account, the better.

QUESTIONS

• What is the difference between the gift of miracles and the gift of healing?

• Have you ever observed a concrete example of this gift being exercised? If so, what effect did it have on you?

THE GIFT OF PRAYER

The gift of prayer belongs to those gifts that the Bible does not explicitly label as "spiritual gifts." Yet, experience demonstrates that there are Christians who have a unique power in prayer. While it is every Christian's privilege and duty to pray, those with this gift are able to spend many hours praying intensively, and they enjoy every minute of it.

SCRIPTURE REFERENCES

Daniel 6:11–12, Daniel 9:1–4, **Luke 11:1–13**, Acts 16:19–34, Colossians 4:12–13, 1 Timothy 2:1–4, James 5:16–18

POSSIBLE TASKS

Prayer groups, leading prayer vigils, spiritual warfare, prayer chains, intercession for specific requests, prayer ministry at specific events ...

THIS GIFT ENABLES YOU TO PRAY FOR CONCRETE REQUESTS OVER LONG PERIODS OF TIME, AND TO RECEIVE VISIBLE ANSWERS FAR MORE FREQUENTLY THAN OTHERS.

DANGERS

- Some Christians with this gift give those without it a guilty conscience, causing them to feel as if they were less spiritual.

- Some prayer warriors with many experiences of answered prayer tend to see "prayer" as an alternative to "action."

TIPS FOR TRAINING THIS GIFT

- Collect a list of specific prayer concerns from your church. Keep track of the requests in a notebook, allowing space to record how and when the request was answered.

- Set aside a specific time every day for prayer. Look for a time period every year for more extended fasting and prayer.

- Set aside a "prayer point" in your home. Take the necessary measures to ensure that you will not be disturbed by the telephone, people, etc.

QUESTIONS

- Do you regard prayer to be work, or is it rather relaxing for you? Describe the feelings you had during your last extended prayer time.

- When you hear of people who spend many hours a day in prayer, do you react more positively, or negatively? Why?

THE GIFT OF PROPHECY

THIS GIFT ENABLES YOU TO RECEIVE A MESSAGE FROM GOD BY THE HOLY SPIRIT AND TO COMMUNICATE IT TO OTHER PEOPLE.

In contrast to common usage, the gift of prophecy does not only refer to the foretelling of future events. Instead, it enables people to serve as the vehicle for a divine message regarding a concrete situation. Please notice that some Christians use terms like "word of knowledge," "word of wisdom", "image," or "vision" for what is referred to here as the gift of prophecy.

SCRIPTURE REFERENCES

Deuteronomy 13:1–5, Deuteronomy 18:18–22, 1 Samuel 3:1–21, Matthew 7:15–20, Matthew 24:11 and 23–24, Acts 15:32, 1 Corinthians 12:28–29, 1 Corinthians 14:3 and 22–40, 2 Peter 1:19–21, **1 John 4:1–6**, Revelation 1:1–3

POSSIBLE TASKS

Foreign missions, evangelistic events, long-term planning, outreach to the underprivileged, worship team, prayer team, small groups, counseling, prayer chains ...

DANGERS

- People with this gift should not evade criticism. In fact, the Bible teaches that prophets must be tested by the church (1 Cor. 14:29).
- Those who have only had this gift a short time sometimes have difficulty determining for whom their prophecy is intended—for themselves, for the church, or for another group.

TIPS FOR TRAINING THIS GIFT

- If you haven't had much experience with this gift, share your messages with Christians who have the gift of discernment, preferably in written form.
- Anyone exercising this gift must acquire a solid biblical foundation in order to better distinguish between divine inspiration and one's own favorite ideas.
- Inform yourself of current social trends. The more informed you are, the more God can use you to speak to certain situations.

QUESTIONS

- What do you think of the following thesis: "Whenever our pastor preaches on Sunday morning, the gift or prophecy is being practiced"?
- Some Christians make the following assertion: "Since the completion of the New Testament, there is no longer any need for the gift of prophecy; and, as a result, it no longer exists." How do you react to this statement?

THE GIFT OF SUFFERING

The gift of suffering involves more than just a willingness to follow Christ to the point of death, although this may be included. While everyone experiences pain and suffering at times, God endows certain people with a special ability to maintain a victorious mindset, even in the midst of intense suffering. The familiar phrase "the blood of the martyrs is the seed of the church" expresses well the relationship between this spiritual gift and church growth.

SCRIPTURE REFERENCES

Matthew 5:10–12, **Acts 7:54–60,** Acts 8:1–4, Acts 20:22–24, Acts 21:4–14, 1 Corinthians 13:1–3, 2 Corinthians 1:8–11, 2 Corinthians 11:21b–33, 2 Corinthians 12:9–10, Philippians 1:12–14, 1 Peter 2:20–25, 1 Peter 4:12–16

THIS GIFT ENABLES YOU TO SUFFER FOR THEIR FAITH WHILE AT THE SAME TIME MAINTAINING A JOYFUL, VICTORIOUS SPIRIT.

POSSIBLE TASKS

Intercession, foreign missions, pioneer ministry ...

DANGERS

- Some people with the gift of suffering expect others who don't have this gift to be willing to take enormous risks—another example of gift projection (see page 87).

- There is a phenomenon that psychology refers to as the "martyr complex." This must be carefully distinguished from the gift of suffering.

- One of the most difficult obstacles for those with this gift is the role that friends pose. Well-meaning friends will often try to protect them from dangerous situations, thus hindering them from doing God's will.

TIPS FOR TRAINING THIS GIFT

- Don't avoid politically dangerous situations just because others lack faith or see insurmountable problems.

- Pursue your personal relationship with God so that it remains vibrant, providing you with extra reserves to draw from in times of suffering.

QUESTIONS

- The Greek word *martys* can be translated either "martyr" or "witness." What is the relationship between these two words?

- Do you know people whose suffering has strengthened your own faith?

THE GIFT OF TONGUES

The gift of tongues comes in two different variations, either as personal prayer or as a public utterance. The second variation should only be exercised with an interpreter (1 Cor. 14:27–28). Caution: In the *Three-Color Gift Test,* the gift of tongues is treated in the same way as all of the other gifts. People who only occasionally pray in tongues will probably not find tongues among their manifest gifts. It will only occur as a manifest gift if speaking in tongues is a significant part of one's spiritual life.

THIS GIFT ENABLES YOU TO USE A LANGUAGE THEY HAVE NEVER LEARNED, EITHER IN THEIR PERSONAL PRAYER TIMES OR FOR A PUBLIC MESSAGE.

SCRIPTURE REFERENCES

Mark 16:17, Acts 2:1–13, Acts 10:44–48, **Acts 19:1–7,** Romans 8:26–27, 1 Corinthians 12:10 and 28–30, 1 Corinthians 14:4–6 and 26–28

POSSIBLE TASKS

Prayer ministry, spiritual warfare ...

DANGERS

• Some people who pray in tongues are ashamed of their gift. They would never admit to others that God has given it to them.

• Speaking in tongues is listed among the most frequently projected spiritual gifts (see page 87). Some people with this gift view it as so natural and simple that they tell others, "You can do it as well, if you only want to."

• Some of the groups which understand speaking in tongues as the trademark of the "baptism of the Holy Spirit," belittle the spiritual authority of Christians who don't have this gift.

TIPS FOR TRAINING THIS GIFT

• If you have this gift, use it frequently, especially during your personal prayer times. Many Christians report how this gift develops with time and increased use.

• Many Christians have had positive experiences utilizing this gift in the context of spiritual warfare.

QUESTIONS

• In your opinion, why do some Christians insist that the gift of tongues doesn't exist today?

• Could the gift of tongues be useful in your own spiritual life?

FREQUENTLY

ASKED

QUESTIONS

The approach to spiritual gifts that is presented in this book has generated considerable discussion. The following questions and answers are, for the most part, based on recordings of spiritual gifts seminars, as well as letters and e-mails that I have received in recent years. Since these questions and answers originated in real-life situations, I have tried to preserve their "live" character for this book.

CHURCHES DON'T WANT TO CHANGE

You suggest that churches which are, for example, strong in the green area, but weak in the blue or red areas should strive to move into these "new areas." But most of the churches I'm aware of have no desire whatsoever to do this. They are proud of what they are, and they might even regard the other colors as threatening.

THE OVERWHELM- ING MAJORITY OF CHURCHES I'M FAMILIAR WITH ARE INTERESTED IN DISCOVERING NEW HORIZONS.

I know some churches like that, too. If there is no wish to improve, the kind of qualitative growth that I am speaking about will not happen. When I work with a church like this, my message is, "You have to make the decision about what is good for you, not I." Of course, I prefer churches that are eager to learn new things and that are open to moving into areas in which they are not yet strong, even when that implies leaving their comfort zone. I am convinced that such an attitude, whether on the part of individual believers or whole churches, is more biblical, more attractive and more joyful than the static opinion, "There is absolutely nothing that I could possibly learn in the future."

However, I don't agree that *most* churches are like this. The overwhelming majority of churches I'm familiar with are eager to learn and interested in discovering new horizons. The good news is that none of us has to give up those areas of strength in which we feel comfortable. The real question is simply this: "Are there some underdeveloped areas which, if improved, would make us more empowered, more obedient, more fulfilled, and more effective?" I don't believe that this kind of question is so threatening.

COLOR SCHEME DOESN'T MATCH REALITY

Your scheme with the three colors looks quite convincing at first sight, but it simply doesn't match reality. For example, I know of a typical liberal (according to your scenario, he would be part of the green segment) who is a rather "controlling believer" (which would be a typical danger for the color red). I myself belong to a charismatic church (blue color), but I discovered in your test that I am a "burned-out believer" (which would imply that I am weak in the blue area). The same holds true for many other individuals in my church.

What you are describing is quite frequently the case. Even if within different Christian traditions there are certain tendencies toward one or two of the colors, this does not mean that every single believer within a certain tradition fits his or her church's color scheme. For instance, not all members of an evangelical church are exclusively strong in the red area; not all charismatics are strong in the blue; and not all liberals are strong in the green. Life isn't like that, and I thank God for this! I even know of entire charismatic churches whose greatest deficiency is in the blue area, and of evangelical churches that are strongest in the green area, and so on. If a church gets such a result, it is important to interpret it carefully. Your interpretation should be as colorful as life itself—not black and white. In assessing such results, you need to keep in mind the distinction between the theological orientation and the actual life of the church. Our three color scheme is applied in both ways and this contributes a lot to these interesting results.

DIFFERENT COLORS IN DIFFERENT TESTS

In the Character Compass, I've identified wisdom (green segment) as my greatest deficiency. On the other hand, four of my five manifest gifts are in the green area: hospitality, mercy, artistic creativity, and music. How does this fit together?

Quite well! You shouldn't expect to identify the same colors in every test. There are, for instance, Christians who have gifts in the blue area, but whose greatest deficiency is power. Other Christians have gifts in the red area, but lack commitment. Still others have gifts in the green area, but are not at all wise. The *Three-Color Gift Test* and the *Character Compass* are two different instruments. The first one tells you what to do, the second one suggests how to do it. Sometimes the color of your gifts in the *Three-Color Gift Test* and the color of your greatest strength in the *Character Compass* match, sometimes they don't. Whatever your personal results are, you can learn much by comparing the two results.

STRENGTHS AND WEAKNESSES OF ENTIRE CONTINENTS

I have listened carefully to your teaching on the different starting points. It was interesting that you illustrated each of the six starting points with an example from a different continent. For the skeptical believer you took an example from Europe; for the controlling believer, an example from Australia; for the spiritualizing believer, an example from Latin America; for the burned-out believer, an example from North America; for the fanatical believer, an example from Asia; and for the detached believer, an example from Africa. Is this just a coincidence, or is there a deeper meaning behind it? Do you see certain tendencies in different continents? To me, this categorization looks a little bit artificial.

YOUR INTERPRETA-TION SHOULD BE AS COLORFUL AS LIFE ITSELF, NOT BLACK AND WHITE.

You are a sharp observer! In the past few years, I have collected many different examples from very different cultures. When I thought about which of these examples could be helpful for illustrating the six starting points, I deliberately took them from the six continents. I actually have the impression—this term is the most precise I can use right now—that there are tendencies toward different colors in different continents. By "tendency" I mean that the number of people with a specific starting point in a given culture is somewhat higher than in another culture. It does *not* mean that every single believer in this particular culture displays this tendency. All six starting points can be found on all continents, probably even in every single church. However, as we do more research in the next few years, we will be able to determine if there really are these tendencies in different cultures, or if this is just an "impression." All of the examples that I give in my teaching are, of course, authentic. So Gordon, Michael, Lucía, Cathy, Sulastri, and Ndoze are real people, just as Thomas, Martha, Mary, Moses, Peter, and Jonah were. In some cases, however, I have changed their names so that they are not identifiable, for obvious reasons.

SEPARATION OF COLORS

In your three-color teaching you separate three dimensions that really belong inextricably together. You speak more about the distinctives of the colors than about what all of them have in common.

I agree that these dimensions belong together, but I don't think that the use of our tools furthers their separation. I can demonstrate that just the opposite holds true. Instead of speaking exclusively about some ideal, but unrealistic state, I want to start where people actually are. Most believers and churches are somewhat out of balance. In such a situation it is no help merely to preach that all three colors belong inextricably together. Rather, we have to show practical ways in which we can move from a situation in which the colors are out of balance, to one in which there is greater equilibrium. I don't want to be among those who are very good at describing how the Christian faith could or should be, but don't offer any direction for how to get there.

WHAT QUALIFIES AS A SPIRITUAL GIFT?

It is perplexing to me that you define all 30 gifts in your book as "spiritual gifts." You should reserve this term only for those gifts that you list in the blue area. Only those are supernatural and thus, spiritual gifts.

If this is the terminology you would like to use, you are free to do so. Here are the reasons that I opted for the terminology that you find in this book. To begin with, I don't believe it would reflect biblical usage to limit the application of the term "spiritual gift" only to those gifts in the blue area. That limitation reflects a misunderstanding of what makes a gift "spiritual." The blue category is indeed a special category, but so are the red and green categories. There are special characteristics that the gifts listed in each of the three categories have in common which set them apart from the gifts in the other categories. For instance, in the blue area there is, without a doubt, a stronger interest in that which transcends rationality. However, what makes a gift "spiritual" is not whether it is more or less overtly transrational. I have difficulty understanding how practicing mercy (green area) or evangelism (red area) could be less spiritual, for instance, than speaking in tongues (blue area).

> IT HAS BEEN MY EXPERIENCE THAT COUNTLESS CHRISTIANS REGARD THE DISCOVERY OF THEIR GIFTS TO BE A KEY EVENT IN THEIR SPIRITUAL JOURNEY.

TEACHING ON SPIRITUAL GIFTS IS OVER-EMPHASIZED

In reading through your book, I get the impression that the most important aspect of the Christian life is discovering one's spiritual gifts. Aren't you placing too much emphasis on this area?

The discovery of one's spiritual gifts is certainly not the most important element in the Christian life. The fact that so much attention is given to it is simply that one of the goals of this book is to help Christians identify their gifts. Other tools focus on other aspects of the Christian life. However, in recent years I've noticed a tremendous need to make up lost ground in this area. Consequently, it is possible that the theme of "gift discovery" could become the primary focus of a church for a given time, before the focus is changed to other areas of ministry. I personally view this as quite normal. It has been my experience that countless Christians regard the discovery of their gifts as a key event in their spiritual journey. My own spiritual pilgrimage confirms this as well.

PSYCHOLOGY INSTEAD OF THE BIBLE

I've never found any sort of Three-Color Gift Test anywhere in Scripture, and it seems to me that at the time the New Testament was written, churches grew quite successfully. The same holds true when we study church history. Were our forefathers misled in never recognizing their "manifest" or "latent" gifts? I'm forced to conclude that your tools are more oriented to modern psychological testing than to the Bible.

I sense the irony of your question and would like to answer openly. Christians of all generations, throughout different time periods, have been discovering their gifts in a variety of ways. Even today, there are a vast number of different methods that can accomplish the same purpose. This is, however, no reason to scrap the approach of this book. In New Testament times there were no newspapers or magazines, no smartphones or computers, nor were there books as we know them today, and the church of Jesus Christ developed quite well. Does that mean that we, as people of the third millennium, have to reject all of these tools? Hardly. Christians claiming this represent a rather adventurous sort of biblicism. Today we live in an age, as you have rightly pointed out, in which a variety of tests have been developed—they have even become quite fashionable. The tests in themselves are neither good nor evil; the question is solely, for what are they used?

IN NEW TESTAMENT TIMES THERE WERE NO RADIOS OR TELEVISIONS, AND THE CHURCH OF JESUS CHRIST DEVELOPED QUITE WELL. DOES THAT MEAN THAT WE, AS PEOPLE OF THE THIRD MILLENNIUM, HAVE TO REJECT ALL OF THESE TOOLS?

THE DANGER OF PRIDE

Don't you think that discovering one's spiritual gifts can lead Christians to pride?

This is a very real danger, and the best—as well as most biblical—protection against this is to integrate people who have discovered their gifts into a permanent ministry. The daily challenges of ministry will very likely dissolve any pride. I suspect, however, that hidden behind a reticence to discover one's gifts is often a much more refined kind of pride. Imagine the following situation: You've bought a valuable present for your neighbor. You present it to her and eagerly await her response. Day after day, she offers no reaction. What's worse, when someone else asks what she thinks of the gift, she says, "I didn't receive any present from my neighbor. I'm much too humble for that." You'd probably ask yourself, "What's come over this woman?" It would never even cross your mind that such a response has anything to do with humility. You'd probably reconsider whether you would ever want to give a present to such an ungrateful person again.

God is in a position in which he's constantly the victim of such responses. He's given each of us as Christians at least one gift, and then he has to listen to the recipients of these gifts deny that they ever received anything—all the while claiming that they are too "humble." This false humility appears to me to be a tremendous obstacle for healthy spiritual growth.

SO MUCH NEVER GETS DONE

Your book was well received in our church. Yet, I see a great danger if everyone only applies him or herself in the areas in which they are gifted. That would mean that a great deal of ministry never is accomplished. Is that what you are advocating?

IF THERE ARE NO CHURCH MEMBERS WITH THE CORRESPONDING GIFTS, IT IS BETTER TO LEAVE THOSE TASKS UNATTENDED.

Let me be perfectly frank. That's exactly what I endorse. If there are no church members who have the corresponding gifts to accomplish certain tasks, it is better to leave those tasks unattended until someone steps forward who does have the necessary gifts. I have to admit that some time ago I would have reacted much differently. I used to say, "Of course, if there are no Christians with the appropriate gifts, then others who don't have the gifts must pinch hit." However, since then I've noticed that this answer, as warmly as it was received by many groups, led in the wrong direction.

I met a pastor not long ago who told me what blessing he's experienced since applying the concept of gift-based ministry in a radical way. Every task is assigned to a person for two years at most. Once this time period comes to an end, there is a "month of reevaluation." During this entire month all church activities, with the exception of the regular worship services, are canceled completely and the volunteer's sole task is to evaluate his or her past term's service. They are to ask, "Does this ministry relate to my gifting?" Anyone who answers this question negatively is encouraged to step down from his or her ministry, even if no replacement is found. This pastor told me, "When we can't find anyone with the necessary gifting to fill a particular slot, we don't just look for a warm body to fill the gap. Instead, we leave the position vacant until someone with the necessary gift steps forward. To try to coerce someone who lacks the appropriate gifting to take on a task is, in my estimation, an affront to the will of God."

It is interesting that since this church has adopted the principle of gift-based ministry, and has found the courage to leave holes in certain areas of ministry, it has experienced significant growth, and *more* tasks have been completed than ever before. These tasks are not necessarily the tasks which were previously regarded as indispensable, but they are certainly the ones that God has willed.

DEEP HURTS

I share your view that people should only assume a task when they have the corresponding gifts. However, according to this standard, I must admit that many people in our church are serving in the wrong place for them to minister effectively. Some of the leaders who had worked through your book communicated this very openly to these people, which led to deep hurts. Just how does one tell others in a softer, more sensitive way that they are not really suited for their current ministry?

I can't emphasize strongly enough that we don't do people a favor by allowing them to stay in a ministry for which they are not suited, simply because we don't want to hurt their feelings. That's one of the most unmerciful things you can do. These people suffer from having to carry out the responsibility, and the people under their care suffer as well. There really is no other solution: Christians involved in ministries that don't match their gifting must be released from those responsibilities.

Once this becomes clear, it is time to consider very carefully how best to communicate this to them. In most instances, the people carrying out the wrong ministries are not to blame for the situation. Perhaps the church leadership failed in not sharing with them the concept of gift-based ministry. Or perhaps they were encouraged to continue in the respective ministry area by those who commended them for their sacrificial service, making them into a kind of martyr: "Just look at the way Jane so willingly offers her time and energy to the children's ministry, even though everyone knows she really can't stand to be around children." When a person grows up in this kind of atmosphere, and is suddenly confronted with the possibility that God's design is something completely different, it can understandably result in deep hurts. For this reason, I would like to propose the following: Before we try to point out to others that their gifts don't match their current ministries, we should make sure they know what their gifts are and only then should we suggest some other ministry options. Once this foundation is laid, the option of stepping back from the familiar, yet less appropriate tasks, can become a positive and encouraging spiritual experience.

BEFORE WE TRY TO POINT OUT TO OTHERS THAT THEIR GIFTS DON'T MATCH THEIR CURRENT MINISTRY, WE SHOULD MAKE SURE THEY KNOW WHAT THEIR GIFTS ARE.

"IF-IT-FEELS-GOOD-DO-IT" MENTALITY

According to your definition, a gift is something that is most fun for me. With this mindset, you're only encouraging a trend which is already far too widespread, namely, that people only pursue what they like to do.

I never said that a spiritual gift is what is most fun for you. To enjoy a certain task is simply one of seven criteria which should be taken into consideration in the discovery process. It is a fact, however, that the tasks to which God calls us by giving us the appropriate gifting will ultimately prove to be the most fulfilling. There is an important distinction to be made here. I am not suggesting that you perpetually ask yourself whether it gets you excited when someone asks you to pursue a specific ministry. In my opinion, this kind of mindset would be inconsistent with what Jesus requires of us. Instead, I'm suggesting that everyone should discover their gifts, and that enjoyment of the corresponding task is an important criterion in the discovery process. Once you've discovered your gifts, concentrate on the tasks

related to them. The issue then becomes not so much what you would like to do in a given moment (feelings can prove to be a fickle standard of measure), but what it means to be faithful to your ministry.

JOY IS NO CRITERION

If it is true that joy is a deciding principle in discovering one's calling, then many leaders throughout church history would never have been called. When I review the biographies of great men and women of faith, there is not a whole lot of evidence of this principle of joy.

Unfortunately, you are right in your last statement. Most of the biographies I have read are not written from the perspective of spiritual gifts. In fact, many Christian biographies seem to be written on the premise that a person who is ill-suited for a ministry or suffers while serving the Lord must have God on his or her side. I suspect that biographers who have this perspective tend to stretch the truth somewhat in an attempt to edify the reader.

It is safe to assume that most of the great heroes of the faith, who presumably lived contrary to their gifting and all that could produce joy, actually *did* live in accordance with their gifting—and *therefore* became heroes. Please don't misunderstand me. There are examples in which God calls people to tasks which don't seem to suit their gifting. Consider Moses, whom God called to challenge Pharaoh to let his people go. However, these appear to be exceptions to the rule. If we want to develop guidelines for our spiritual lives, it's important to stress the rules rather than the exceptions.

SIXTY-TWO PERCENT OF ALL TEST-TAKERS INDICATED THAT THE TEST HELPED THEM DISCOVER NEW GIFTS.

RECEIVING RATHER THAN DISCOVERING ONE'S GIFTS

You're talking about how important it is to discover one's gifts, whereas the real issue is asking God for gifts, and then receiving them from him.

Actually both dimensions are important. You're right that this book does indeed suggest first and foremost that we discover the gifts God has already given to us. That is the first step.

If it's true that every Christian has at least one gift (which is the teaching of the New Testament), and if it's true that 80 percent of Christians do not know what gifts they possess, then we should discover which gifts we already have before we ask God to give us new ones. But apart from that, I would agree that we should always be open to new gifts that God may want to give us. It's my conviction, however, that this is a second step. Why should I ask God for new gifts when I'm not even using the gifts he's already given me?

In some of my gifts seminars, I try to tie these two steps together. During the first part, for instance, I assist the participants in discovering their spiritual gifts by using the *Three-Color Gift Test*. In the second part, which we spend primarily in prayer, we may ask God for new gifts. This combination seems to me to be quite healthy. In a way, it tries to combine all three colors in our diagram.

INCREASINGLY MORE COMPLEX

In previous editions of this book the readers were simply helped to discover their most developed spiritual gifts—no more, no less. I wished you would return to this initial simplicity. I don't need all of this sophisticated three-color information.

If your goal is exclusively to identify your—and other persons—most developed gifts, the present system will give you exactly that kind of information, and it will be accessible to you quicker and more precisely than ever before. If you are not interested in additional information, for instance an evaluations based on the three colors, you can simply disregard those parts. However, there are readers, and they are the overwhelming majority, who appreciate particularly this additional information. But nobody is forced to deal with it. In other words, you can still utilize the test in exactly the same way as you have done it in the past.

WHY SHOULD I ASK GOD FOR NEW GIFTS WHEN I'M NOT EVEN USING THE GIFTS HE'S ALREADY GIVEN ME?

The same applies to all building blocks of Natural Church Development. We are thankful that today we can offer many more tools than ten years ago. However, that does not imply that every church has to use all of these resources. The tools are deliberately designed systemically: All of us can enter the process where it makes most sense for us, and all of us can decide ourselves if we want to work with a respective tool, and to what level we want to work with it.

NOTHING NEW DISCOVERED

The Three-Color Gift Test only served to confirm the gifts I already knew I had. This is nice, but not particularly helpful.

A number of people have told me that this has been their experience. It only makes sense that if you already know what your gifts are, the *Three-Color Gift Test* won't reveal much to you that is new. Some people, however, who believed they could identify their gifts quite definitively, experienced some surprises in using this tool. Sixty-two percent of all test takers indicated that the *Three-Color Gift Test* helped them discover new gifts; 81 percent said that the test confirmed gifts they already knew they had; 6 percent recorded that the test yielded faulty results; and 2 percent suggested that the tool didn't help them at all. Thus, the composite indicates that the *Three-Color Gift Test* will confirm existing gifts and also make you aware of new gifts.

WHAT ARE LATENT GIFTS?

You speak of latent gifts. First of all, it strikes me that this term cannot be found anywhere in the Bible. Second, what do you actually mean by latent gifts? Are they gifts which God may well have given us, but which have remained hidden over a long period of time? Or are they areas in which God will give us new gifts in the future? Or are they areas in which I simply have a higher level of awareness than others, which in reality have nothing to do with spiritual gifts whatsoever?

It could actually be any of these three possibilities. The questions for latent gifts focus on personal desire, our sensitivity to need in an area of ministry, and a willingness to use the gift in question. Answering all three questions positively does not necessarily mean that a spiritual gift is indeed present. At the same time, I have observed how God more often gives new gifts in areas in which these three "symptoms" show up. If this happens, is this then a newly *endowed,* or a newly *discovered* gift? Well, I don't know if it is really possible to answer this question. However, an answer to it wouldn't have any practical consequences for you anyway.

We have introduced the concept of "latent gifts" to open our eyes to areas in which we might expect changes in the future. As far as "manifest gifts" are concerned, we can base our answers exclusively on our previous experience. If you've never been active in a particular area of ministry, the *Three-Color Gift Test* cannot indicate that you

MANY PEOPLE ARE SKEPTICAL OF TESTS IN WHICH THEY CAN'T IDENTIFY WHICH FACTORS INFLUENCE THE RESULT.

have the corresponding gift even though God might have given this gift to you long ago. Thus, analyzing your desires, sensitivity to need, and willingness to use the gift is a good springboard, not only for reflecting on the past, but also for looking ahead to possible future developments.

MISLEADING RESULTS

When I took the Three-Color Gift Test, I came up with completely wrong test results. How do you explain that?

There are two possible explanations: either there is something wrong with the test, or there is something wrong with your opinion about the results. We should be open to either option. There are cases in which the test, for whatever reason, may yield inaccurate results. My experience has shown, however, that in most cases where people have difficulty accepting the results, God may be trying to show them something new.

Allow me to illustrate. While we were still developing the questionnaire, a young man named Frank completed the test and his primary manifest gift was that of missionary. He approached me with this result and remarked, rather ironically, "Christian, here's proof that your tool is really misleading. I was born in Spain, grew up in Mexico, and then moved to Germany, spending most of my life in foreign cultures. No wonder it's easy for me to adapt to a foreign culture. But that has absolutely nothing to do with my spiritual gifting and calling."

Sometime later I tried to contact Frank, which proved to be quite a challenge. I discovered that he had moved from Germany to Hong Kong. Since our conversation, Frank had discovered that God had indeed given him the gift of missionary, and he had acted on this new insight without delay. I had the opportunity to talk with him when he returned to Germany for furlough and he told me, "At first, I really resisted the idea that God might want me to serve as a missionary. Yet, the more I thought about it and prayed for God's will, the clearer it became to me that this really was God's call for my life. Among other things, God had been preparing me for this step through my experience of growing up in foreign cultures."

POSSIBLE DANGERS

It certainly sounds modest for you to admit that the Three-Color Gift Test may yield inaccurate scores with some individuals, but that's still a rather general statement. Give us some concrete examples in which the test unquestionably produced wrong scores.

Certainly. There are examples of misleading results among those test takers who have psychological or social disorders. For instance, some people have problems with interpersonal relationships. Since interpersonal problems often manifest themselves in relation to a potential life partner, some people produce test scores that inaccurately suggest that they have the gift of singleness. Or take the gift of helps. Some Christians suffer from "helper's syndrome," and it's most probable that they will answer the questions in such a way that the gift of helps appears among their manifest gifts. What is even worse is that these people may then conduct themselves in a manner that only serves to increase their problem. These are all issues that I address in my comments on the various gifts, but that this book alone cannot solve. Such people need counseling and companionship to work through these issues.

Admittedly, sometimes it is not that easy to distinguish between helper's syndrome and the gift of helps, or between those who have relational difficulties and those who have the gift of singleness, or even a martyr complex and the gift of suffering. There are cases in which helper's syndrome is suspected, but in reality the gift of helps is being exercised in a marvelous way. To achieve clarity in such cases, a high degree of sensitivity is necessary.

DOES GOD RESCIND GIFTS?

You stated that gifts are intended to be used permanently. Aren't there examples of God taking back gifts?

While this may occur, it is the exception, and not the rule. Seldom does God retract gifts, even when they are clearly misused. God distributes gifts according to his grace, not according to our maturity or personal integrity. For this reason, one should assume that once a gift is discovered and confirmed, it can be used permanently.

WE HAVE INTRODUCED THE CONCEPT OF "LATENT GIFTS" TO OPEN OUR EYES TO AREAS IN WHICH WE MIGHT EXPECT CHANGES IN THE FUTURE.

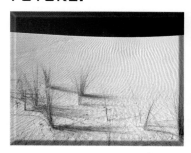

DIFFERING RESULTS EVERY TIME

I've taken the test a number of times and each time I have come up with a somewhat different result. How do you explain that?

This is a common experience for those who complete the questionnaire a number of times. There are a couple of explanations for this. First, the circumstances you are in when completing the questionnaire have a great impact on how you answer the questions. If your situation changes, you may answer the questions differently and thus get a different result. Second, it may also be possible that God wants to draw your attention to a specific gift through changes between two test scores. I have observed this a number of times.

Take Maria, for instance, who I met at a seminar. She had completed the questionnaire three times within two years. The first time, "evangelism" had not appeared in her gift mix; the second time, it was ranked fourth; the third time, it had moved to first. It seemed that God was leading Maria into an evangelistic ministry over time, and was equipping her with the corresponding gift. It is important for us to be open to changes. I've noticed in my own life how my awareness of God's leading grows as I repeat the *Three-Color Gift Test* at regular intervals.

EXPERIMENTING IS DANGEROUS

You talk about "experimenting" with gifts, and it sounds good initially, but there are some serious dangers in this. I don't think it's wise to experiment with spiritual things without some precautions.

You're right. I admit that I have underestimated these dangers in the past when counseling others to "try it out, and see what happens." One event that really left me thinking about this issue occurred during a gifts seminar in Switzerland. After I had spoken on the topic of "experimenting as much as possible," a woman in a wheelchair approached me during the break and said, "It was hard for me to agree with you. I've heard those words in a number of different contexts at Christian gatherings and then, during the prayer times, people have come to me with the intention of discovering whether they have the gift of healing." She then told me stories of situations which proved to be rather traumatic for her. As I imagined these people all experimenting on her because of what I had suggested, I felt deeply rebuked.

IF I'VE NEVER BEEN ACTIVE IN A PARTICULAR AREA OF MINISTRY, THE *THREE-COLOR GIFT TEST* CANNOT INDICATE WHETHER I HAVE THE CORRESPONDING GIFT.

There are gifts that are relatively easy to experiment with, and others which should be tried out only under the direction of a more mature individual possessing this gift. This is the best protection against some irrational action that can lead to spiritual harm. However, even with this emphasis on safeguards, I would like to encourage experimentation. Most churches are simply too cautious. The fear of failure appears to me to be inappropriate, especially for Christians seeking to discover their giftedness. I'm advocating that churches provide an open climate where people can joyously experiment, risk failure, and learn from their mistakes.

LITTLE OPPORTUNITY TO USE ONE'S GIFTS

In my church there is hardly any opportunity to utilize my gifts. Do people in other churches express similar frustrations?

It can indeed be frustrating to discover that one has certain gifts and then find no outlet to use them. Some Christians are less content after discovering their gifts than they were beforehand. I once had someone tell me, "When I didn't know my gifts, I was quite happy. But now that I know what I should be doing but can't, I am frustrated."

Let me share two recommendations for anyone who faces a similar situation. First, determine *why* the use of your gifts is not welcomed in your church. It could be that the leadership has the impression that you're not ready to use this gift in a responsible way or that there are other concerns that may have more to do with your character or maturity, rather than your gifts. When it comes to accomplishing tasks in a church, the criterion of spiritual gifts is not only important, it is indispensable; but there are other criteria as well. There are often legitimate reasons why the exercise of certain gifts is not encouraged by church leaders.

Second, should you come to the conclusion that the reason this gift is not encouraged is anything but a spiritual reason, I suggest you look for an alternative. If you can't grow spiritually and use your spiritual gifts in your church, and a discussion with the leadership doesn't change the situation, then you should ask God to direct you to another church. Make sure, however, that you are consistent with your new commitment. I am not encouraging the all-too-common practice of church hopping.

IT MAY BE THAT GOD WANTS TO DRAW YOUR ATTENTION TO A SPECIFIC GIFT THROUGH CHANGES BETWEEN TWO TEST SCORES.

WHEN CERTAIN GIFTS ARE LACKING

You said that some people find it hard to talk about gifts they don't have, yet that seems perfectly normal to me. Who wants to talk about his or her shortcomings?

Sorry, but the second part of your question indicates that you are operating from a misunderstanding. It is not a shortcoming to discover that you do not have certain gifts. Rather, it is a further step in your discovery process. Each time you discover a gift you don't have, it is a reason to celebrate. As a result of this discovery, you will know more about what God is, and is not calling you to. When I say that each gift that we don't have is a reason to celebrate, I mean this literally. When a person progresses to that point, they have made great strides in comprehending what the body of Christ is all about.

A RELAXED ATMOSPHERE

We are in the process of working through your book in our home Bible study. As the leader, I am wondering how to create an atmosphere in which others will freely talk about their gifts. Everyone is still rather closed.

I face the same situation every time I lead a gifts seminar. In these seminars, it is not my primary goal that the participants discover their gifts, although typically this is one of the results. My goal is to create an atmosphere in which it is easy for everyone to speak about gifts they do and don't have. Very often when I share about the gifts I do *not* have, and how I came to this discovery, it has an extremely relaxing effect. In so doing, the exaltation of the seminar leader as some kind of "guru" falls apart. It is then easier for the participants to talk about the gifts they do and don't have as well.

What is, and isn't a spiritual gift

I don't understand your gift list. How is it that you've adopted qualities like "singleness," for example, that lack any biblical support?

Included in our list are gifts which the Bible clearly and expressly refers to as *charismata* or "spiritual gifts." Others, such as the gift of missionary, are included because, in the context of Scripture, spiritual gifting appears to be involved. Finally, the list includes gifts which the Bible does not directly refer to as spiritual gifts, but which can be understood in this way (e.g. prayer and deliverance). The gift of singleness, however, clearly belongs in the first category (cf. 1 Cor. 7:7). It is interesting to note that this biblical concept appears so seldom in the literature on spiritual gifts.

Singleness is not a gift

In my opinion, singleness is nothing more than a lack of opportunity. We had a person in our small group who was quite unhappy that she wasn't married. Can you imagine the pain she felt when others suggested she had the gift of singleness? She had no choice but to agree in an attempt to guard her integrity.

There are gifts that are relatively easy to experiment with, and others that should be tried only under the direction of a more mature individual.

Paul clearly regarded his own singleness to be a spiritual gift *(charisma)*, not a lack of opportunity (1 Cor. 7:7). I've met countless Christians in recent years to whom God has given this wonderful gift and who have been using it to the glory of God and for the development of his church. Several have told me how fellow Christians pressured them to "finally get married," apparently unaware that a spiritual calling was behind their singleness. However, not everybody who is single has this gift, and probably the person you are referring to doesn't have it. The manner in which this topic was handled in your group is an example of how not to deal with this question. It disturbs me that apparently there are relatively few groups in which one of its members can openly admit, "Folks, I'm unmarried and I'm not particularly happy about it. I'd like to have a partner, and I struggle with my sexuality." We have to make more of an effort to provide an atmosphere in our small groups in which this kind of open sharing can take place.

Strange definitions

I'm surprised by some of your definitions for the gifts. The way you define the gift of knowledge, for example, is really rather peculiar.

There are certain gifts, and knowledge is one of them, which are understood in different ways within the body of Christ. Scripture does not define the individual gifts, and this leads to a variety of definitions. I'm not suggesting that our definitions (most of which are based on C. Peter Wagner's book on spiritual gifts) are correct, and all others are false. Yet, if we want to speak about a spiritual gift, we must have a clear understanding of how we are defining it. Therefore, I give precise definitions reflecting the way the different gifts have been used in the questionnaire.

I suspect that your church understands the gift of knowledge as a believer receiving a supernatural insight into a specific situation. Only the "supernatural" elements are included; the "natural" parts in the discovery process are excluded. This is a widespread understanding of this gift, especially in charismatic churches. It is certainly one possible way to define it, because the supernatural phenomenon described does exist. If I use the term differently, this does not imply that the phenomenon is not included in the *Three-Color Gift Test,* it is just that I am using terminology in a different way than you are accustomed to. In this book, I don't relate this phenomenon to "knowledge," but to "prophecy." Thus, it is possible that the individual terms I use must be reinterpreted somewhat to fit your specific context.

TONGUES IN THE *THREE-COLOR GIFT TEST*

I have the gift of tongues, but this did not show up as a gift of mine in the Three-Color Gift Test. Does that mean I don't really have this gift?

I have treated this gift as I have all of the others in the test. If you pray in tongues from time to time, yet this is not a basic element of your spiritual life, then tongues will probably not appear as one of your manifest gifts. It will only appear if this gift has a more significant role in your life. This is true of all of the other gifts as well. For instance, I have led others to faith in Christ from time to time, but I don't have the gift of evangelism. I've also seen God answer my prayers for healing on occasion, yet I don't have the gift of healing. Therefore, if tongues is not a significant component of your spiritual life, it won't appear in your manifest gift mix.

CHURCHES SHOULD PROVIDE AN OPEN CLIMATE WHERE PEOPLE CAN JOYOUSLY EXPERIMENT, RISK FAILURE, AND LEARN FROM THEIR MISTAKES.

GIFTS CAN BE ABUSED

There's no doubt in my mind that gifts like tongues and healing are still being exercised today, but you have to admit that these gifts are easily abused. That's why I don't allow any opportunity for them to be exercised in my church.

What is the misuse of a gift? Misuse occurs when a gift is not serving to build up the body of Christ, but rather serves to honor the gift-bearer. This is true of all the gifts, not just the ones that you mentioned. Imagine the awful effect it would have if gifts like teaching, evangelism, or leadership were exercised in order to honor the gift-bearer rather than to build up the church. We shouldn't guard against the misuse of the gifts by prohibiting them, but by demonstrating ways in which they can be properly exercised to edify the church.

A BUILT-IN ONE-SIDEDNESS

A consistent application of one's gifts inevitably leads to one-sidedness. Is it your intention to have people focus more and more on their gifts and ignore the areas that don't match their gifting?

To offer you an unmistakably clear response: Yes, I am hoping that Christians will become one-sided, extreme, and radical in applying their gifts. I am convinced that this is the way the body of Christ functions best. For example, I recommend that Christians who discover they have the gift of evangelism step down from other church responsibilities in order to devote themselves wholeheartedly to evangelistic tasks and opportunities. I could share illustration after illustration of how this "one-sidedness" has resulted in great blessing for the church.

Let me give one example to illustrate this. I met a church board member who had confirmed his gift of evangelism through the *Three-Color Gift Test*. Yet, he was actively involved in so many other activities that he had little time to exercise this gift. His pastor encouraged him to step down from all of his other church responsibilities and focus on evangelism. The pastor later told me, "I nearly had tears in my eyes when he left the board, since he was always the one in the group who promoted evangelistic outreach. It became clear, however, that a person with the gift of evangelism shouldn't be there to promote evangelism, but rather to evangelize. In the last six months, nine new people have become a part of our church because of his ministry."

IS IT WORTH ALL THE BOTHER?

Please tell us how other groups have been helped by the Three-Color Gift Test. Do most churches feel that all this effort pays off?

We asked 214 group leaders who had used the book in their small groups how strong the interest had been. Here are the results: 74 percent answered "exceptionally strong" or "very strong;" 25 percent "moderately strong," and one percent "minimal interest" or "no interest." We then surveyed 623 of the members of these groups to determine whether the book had helped them. Sixty-nine percent answered "very much" or "much;" 27 percent, "to some extent;" and 4 percent, "minimal" or "not at all."

IT'S NOT A SHORT-COMING TO DISCOVER THAT YOU DON'T HAVE CERTAIN GIFTS, BUT RATHER A FURTHER STEP IN YOUR DISCOVERY PROCESS.

THE *THREE-COLOR* GIFT TEST IN YOUTH MINISTRY

Do you recommend the Three-Color Gift Test for youth ministry?

Yes, with certain limitations. I believe we should share the concept of spiritual gifts with teenagers and encourage them to experiment. Because youth are considering career choices, the issue of gifting is all the more relevant for them. Working through the book can prove to be a valuable resource along the way. At the same time, we need to make it clear—even more so than when working with adults—that the test scores are by no means definitive. Premature conclusions can prove to be counterproductive in further personal development.

Another limitation is that the *Three-Color Gift Test* is not specifically written for youth, which means it contains numerous life situations which young people might find inapplicable. The percentage of those who find the test of little help is higher among youth than among adults.

ONLY TO BE CONDUCTED IN GROUPS

In my estimation it is dangerous for an individual who does not belong to a Christian group to conduct the Three-Color Gift Test alone. You should make sure that it is only distributed to groups.

I certainly understand your concern. I would confirm that the *Thee-Color Gift Test* is best used in a group context. This was our primary purpose in developing it. However, I have heard countless stories of how individuals who have used the book outside of a group context have been blessed by God for their efforts.

FRUIT IS MORE IMPORTANT THAN GIFTS

The Bible teaches that the fruit of the Spirit is far more important than the spiritual gifts. Why is there no mention of it in your writing?

There is quite a bit that is foundational to the Christian life that does not appear in this book. This book addresses the issue of discovering one's spiritual gifts. However, I do agree with you wholeheartedly. The New Testament teaches that the gifts of the Spirit without the fruit of the Spirit are, personally, of no value, and our daily experience confirms this. For this reason, we have developed another book in the *NCD Discipleship Resources* series called *The 3 Colors of Love*. This book includes a questionnaire in which the fruit of the Spirit is tested.

MY PRIMARY GOAL IS TO CREATE AN ATMOSPHERE IN WHICH IT IS EASY FOR EVERY PARTICIPANT TO SPEAK ABOUT GIFTS THEY DO AND DON'T HAVE.

THE MOST IMPORTANT GIFTS ARE MISSING

Shouldn't important gifts such as patience, gentleness, and self-control also be included in your gift list?

No! The characteristics you mention are not spiritual gifts. Rather, they belong to the fruit of the Spirit, as mentioned by Paul in Galatians 5:22. In the area of spiritual gifts, we need to concentrate on those we have and not worry about those gifts that we do not have.

This does not apply, however, to the fruit of the Spirit, where it is exactly the other way around. If you discover you are strong in gentleness, but lack patience and self-control, it would be wrong to say, "My fruit is gentleness; other Christians should be exercising patience and self-control." In fact, the aspects of the fruit that are *least* evident in one's life are those that a Christian should seek *most* to develop.

Without the balance of the teaching of the fruit of the Spirit, it is easy for the gift-based approach to become an ideology. It seems to me that Paul maintains a similar viewpoint in emphasizing love as *the* fruit of the Spirit.

HIGH "IDENTITY" ENERGY

When you talked about divine energies, you mentioned that people with high energy for identity should play a key role when it comes to gift-based ministry. What does that approach exactly imply?

Hardly anything addresses the question of who we are and what our unique role in this world should be, more profoundly than identifying our identity as part of the body of Christ. For people who have high identity energy, the discovery and development of their own gifts doesn't only play a more important role than for others, but they usually also love to help others activate their gifts. If leaders are looking out for Christians who can serve as agents for gift-based ministry within their church—and we definitely need these kind of people if we want to see the process become sustainable—they should particularly look for people with high identity energy. Wherever the concept of spiritual gifts is combined with the concept of the divine energies, amazing results can be expected.

DIFFERENCES COMPARED TO OTHER GIFT TESTS

Meanwhile I have collected a number of different gift tests that have been developed by various groups. Could you shortly summarize the features that distinguish your test from others?

For me, the most important features of the *Three-Color Gift Test* that distinguish this tool from other tests, are the following five:

IMAGINE THE AWFUL EFFECT IT WOULD HAVE IF GIFTS LIKE TEACHING, EVANGELISM, OR LEADERSHIP WERE EXERCISED IN ORDER TO HONOR THE GIFTBEARER, RATHER THAN TO BUILD THE CHURCH.

1. To my knowledge, the *Three-Color Gift Test* is based on the most comprehensive list of gifts—30 gifts as a whole. Other tests, I would assume deliberately, work with shorter lists, for instance by avoiding what they see as "charismatic gifts," or a number of the gifts that we have related to the green color spectrum. However, our goal was to develop a procedure that is not bound to one specific spiritual tradition. I find it very encouraging that, to give just a few examples, both Pentecostals and non-charismatics, both Catholics and Protestants, both Westerners and Orientals work with this exact same tool.

2. I don't know exactly how much time, money, and energy other groups have invested in the scientific normation of their tests according to different languages and cultures, but I can say that this topic is for us of utmost importance. This applies to Natural Church Development in general. For us, a high scientific standard in test development is not just an academic question, but an ethical issue. Only by applying these procedures can we expect precise results. The fact that NCD has been implemented in about 70,000 churches worldwide and that we have the data of all of these churches in our computers, enables us to apply procedures that would be difficult for others to replicate. The huge amount of data helps us to distinguish between successful models, on the one hand, and universal principles, on the other.

3. The *Three-Color Gift Test* doesn't only reveal areas of giftedness in which we have gained sufficient practical experiences (the so-called "manifest gifts"), but also draws our attention to areas in which we may make new discoveries in the future (the so-called "latent gifts"). This dynamic understanding that includes openness for new discoveries distinguishes the *Three-Color Gift Test* from approaches that have a tendency to press people into relatively static boxes: "These are your gifts and this will be the reality you have to address until the end of your life."

I AM HOPING THAT CHRISTIANS WILL BECOME ONE-SIDED, EXTREME, AND RADICAL IN APPLYING THEIR GIFTS.

4. Another typical feature of the *Three-Color Gift Test* is the fact that it is an integral part of Natural Church Development. Of course, everyone can take the test, even if he or she may not be interested in the other elements. But whenever an individual or a group wants to dive deeper into a specific area of church life—for instance, in the area of leadership, small groups, or spirituality—there are always building blocks that supplement the Gift Test, are compatible with it, and build on it. That is particularly of advantage when a whole church works with the respective tools.

5. For me personally, the most important feature is that the *Three-Color Gift Test* approaches the discovery of spiritual gifts as a communal process. This is stressed by external questionnaires, the possibility to share one's results with others, the offer of group profiles, and many more elements.

Because of this unique positioning, *The 3 Colors of Your Gifts* has become internationally the market leader in the area of gift tests. Nevertheless, there are a number of people who prefer other tests (for instance those that work with less gifts, no external questionnaires and no three-color teaching). If you should be one of these people, I would like to expressly encourage you to continue using those tools. We have good reasons why we have developed the test exactly in the form in which the latest version has been published. And other groups have good reasons for designing the tests that they have developed differently.

ANHANG

MINISTRY DESCRIPTION (SEE PAGES 81–83)

Task	Date

Goals

Sub-tasks

Contact people

Responsible for:
Responsible to:
Work with:

Spiritual gifts	Abilities/Interests

Time commitment	Length of assignment

Training

Additional agreements
